W9-ABH-182

ENTIRE FUNCTIONS

BY

A. I. MARKUSHEVICH

Moscow State University

Translated by Scripta Technica, Inc.

Translation Editor: Leon Ehrenpreis
Courant Institute of Mathematical Sciences
New York University

NEW YORK

AMERICAN ELSEVIER PUBLISHING COMPANY INC.

1966

Originally published as
TSELYYE FUNKTII
Nauka Press, Moscow, 1965

SOLE DISTRIBUTORS FOR GREAT BRITAIN
ELSEVIER PUBLISHING COMPANY, LTD.
Barking, Essex, England

SOLE DISTRIBUTORS FOR THE CONTINENT OF EUROPE
ELSEVIER PUBLISHING COMPANY
Amsterdam, The Netherlands

Library of Congress Catalog Card Number: 66-25114

COPYRIGHT © 1966 BY AMERICAN ELSEVIER PUBLISHING COMPANY, INC.

ALL RIGHTS RESERVED. THIS BOOK OR ANY PART THEREOF
MUST NOT BE REPRODUCED IN ANY FORM WITHOUT THE WRITTEN
PERMISSION OF THE PUBLISHER, AMERICAN ELSEVIER PUBLISHING
COMPANY, INC., 52 VANDERBILT AVENUE, NEW YORK, N. Y. 10017

MANUFACTURED IN THE UNITED STATES OF AMERICA

CARLSON

QA
351
,M34tE

Preface

Entire functions are the simplest and most commonly encountered functions. In high school, we encounter both entire
functions (polynomials, the exponential function, the sine and
cosine), and meromorphic functions, that is, the ratios of two
entire functions (rational functions, the tangent and cotangent)
and, finally, the inverse functions of the entire and meromorphic functions (fractional powers, logarithms, the inverse
trigonometric functions).

Entire functions possess many remarkable properties. But
an understanding of the overall theory behind these properties,
to which many specialized books have been devoted, requires a
knowledge of the theory of analytic functions on a university-
course level. The present book does not assume extensive
knowledge of the subject on the part of the reader. Specifically,
the only prerequisite for the greater part of the text is a familiarity with complex numbers and the algebraic operations on
them, and a knowledge of the basic principles of mathematical
analysis (differentiation and integration, the concept of a convergent series).

Obviously, this book does not and can not give an extensively
developed theory of entire functions; this is the task of more
specialized monographs. For the most part, the information
contained here will enable the reader to understand better and
more thoroughly the facts related to an academic course. Here,
we clarify the similarities and differences between what is
algebraic and what is transcendental (from the point of view of
analysis, not number theory). As a heuristic description, we
might say that transcendental entire functions are, both from
the method of defining them and from the rapidity of growth,
"polynomials of infinitely high degree."

For example, consider Picard's "little theorem," which
asserts that the equation $f(x) = A$, where $f(x)$ is a transcendental
entire function and A is a given complex number, has, in general, an infinite set of roots. This theorem may be regarded

III

as the analog of the fundamental theory of algebra, according to which the number of roots of the equation $P(x) = A$, where $P(x)$ is a polynomial, is equal to the degree of the polynomial. Picard's theorem (or more accurately, a modification of it proven in Section 1 of the Appendix) enables us to show that the equation $2^x = Ax$ has an infinite set of roots if $A \neq 0$ and that the equation $\sin x = Ax$ has an infinite set of roots for all A without exception. We show how to find asymptotic expressions for these roots.

We also take up certain algebraic relationships between entire functions (as an extremely simple example, consider the identity $\sin^2 x + \cos^2 x = 1$), periodicity, and algebraic addition theorems (for example, $a^{x_1} a^{x_2} = a^{x_1 + x_2}$).

The culmination of the book is Weierstrass' theorem, which states that entire functions possessing an addition theorem are either algebraic or trigonometric polynomials.

For the convenience of the reader, the book is divided into two parts.

We have tried to make the basic text, consisting of the first five chapters, as accessible as possible, omitting from it the proof of the more difficult theorems. For the most part, this portion is based on two lectures given by the author at Moscow University in the spring of 1962 in courses for teachers.

The other portion, treated as an appendix, contains the proof of Picard's theorem for entire functions of finite order, the expansion of an entire periodic function into a trigonometric series, and Weierstrass' theorem (in a weakened form) regarding entire functions possessing an algebraic addition theorem.

In the first chapter, certain basic propositions in the general theory of analytic functions are formulated without proof. For those who wish a systematic presentation of material in this field, we recommend the books by V. L. Goncharov, *Teoriya funktsiy kompleksnogo peremennogo* (Theory of Functions of a Complex Variable), Uchpedgiz, Moscow, 1955; B. A. Fuks and B. V. Shabat, *Funktsii kompleksnogo peremennogo i nekotoryye ikh prilozheniya* (Functions of a Complex Variable and Certain of their Applications), 2nd ed., Fizmatgiz, Moscow, 1959, or our *Kratkiy kurs teorii analiticheskikh funktsiy* (A Brief Course in the Theory of Analytic Functions), Fizmatgiz, Moscow, 1961, which includes a bibliography for further reading. To this list, we should add the comprehensive book by M. A. Evgrafov, *Asimptoticheskiye otsenki i tselyye funktsii* (Asymptotic Estimates and Entire Functions), 2nd ed., revised, Fizmatgiz, Moscow, 1962.

THE AUTHOR

Contents

The Concept of an
Entire Function

1. A natural generalization of the concept of a polynomial is that of an everywhere-convergent power series.

$$a_0 + a_1 x + a_2 x^2 + \ldots + a_n x^n + \ldots . \tag{1}$$

In such a power series, if all the coefficients beginning with some $(n+1)$st coefficient vanish, we obtain as a special case a polynomial of degree not exceeding n:

$$P(x) = a_0 + a_1 x + \ldots + a_n x^n. \tag{2}$$

A very simple power series that is not everywhere-convergent, one with which we are familiar from school, is the series

$$1 + x + x^2 + \ldots + x^n + \ldots .$$

This series converges only for $|x| < 1$. The coefficients are too large for this series to converge when $|x| \geqslant 1$. (Here, $a_n = 1$ for every n.)

It can be shown that *a power series of the form (1) converges for every x if and only if*

$$\lim_{n \to \infty} \sqrt[n]{|a_n|} = 0. \tag{3}$$

Here, we shall confine ourselves to proving the sufficiency of this condition. For $x = 0$, the series (1) converges. Suppose now that $x \neq 0$. Then, on the basis of condition (3), there exists an N such that the inequality $n > N$ implies the inequality

$$\sqrt[n]{|a_n|} < \frac{1}{2|x|}, \text{ or } |a_n||x^n| < \frac{1}{2^n}.$$

But this means that all the terms in the series (1) are less in absolute value when $n > N$ than the terms of the geometric progression with ratio $1/2$. Therefore, the series (1) converges (in fact converges absolutely).

In what follows, we shall assume that condition (3) is satisfied. Sometimes, it is more convenient to use the simpler sufficient (though, in this case, not necessary) condition for the series (1) to converge everywhere:

$$\lim_{n \to \infty} \frac{a_{n+1}}{a_n} = 0. \tag{3'}$$

This is a sufficient condition because the limit of the ratio of one term to the preceding one in the series (1)

$$a_{n+1}x^{n+1} : a_n x^n = (a_{n+1} : a_n) x$$

(here, we assume that $a_n \neq 0$ and $x \neq 0$) will also be equal to 0 in this case. This implies that the series converges for all x in accordance with d'Alembert's familiar test.

Thus, for example, the series

$$x + \frac{x^2}{2^2} + \frac{x^3}{3^3} + \dots + \frac{x^n}{n^n} + \dots$$

converges everywhere since

$$\lim_{n \to \infty} \sqrt[n]{\frac{1}{n^n}} = \lim_{n \to \infty} \frac{1}{n} = 0.$$

Similarly, the series

$$1 + x + x^2 + \dots + x^n + \dots$$

converges everywhere since

$$\lim_{n \to \infty} \left[\frac{1}{(n+1)!} : \frac{1}{n!} \right] = 0.$$

2. The function representing the limit of an everywhere-convergent power series is called an *entire function*.

Thus, every polynomial is an entire function.

Other examples of entire functions are the exponential function a^x (where $0 < a \neq 1$), and $\cos x$ and $\sin x$. In courses in mathematical analysis, it is shown (with the aid of Taylor's formula) that each of these functions can be represented as the limit of an everywhere-convergent power series:

$$a^x = 1 + \frac{x \ln a}{1!} + \frac{x^2 (\ln a)^2}{2!} + \cdots + \frac{x^n (\ln a)^n}{n!} + \cdots, \tag{4}$$

$$\cos x = 1 - \frac{x^2}{2!} + \frac{x^4}{4!} - \cdots, \tag{5}$$

$$\sin x = x - \frac{x^3}{3!} + \frac{x^5}{5!} - \cdots. \tag{6}$$

In the particular case in which $a = e = 2.71828 \ldots$ (that is, e is the natural logarithm base), we obtain from formula (4)

$$e^x = 1 + \frac{x}{1!} + \frac{x^2}{2!} + \cdots + \frac{x^n}{n!} + \cdots. \tag{4'}$$

With the aid of these formulas, we can obtain a number of other simple examples of entire functions:

$$e^{-x} = 1 - \frac{x}{1!} + \frac{x^2}{2!} - \cdots + (-1)^n \frac{x^n}{n!} + \cdots;$$

$$e^{x^3} = 1 + \frac{x^3}{1!} + \frac{x^6}{2!} + \cdots + \frac{x^{3n}}{n!} + \cdots;$$

$$\frac{e^x - 1 - x}{x^2} = \frac{1}{2!} + \frac{x}{3!} + \frac{x^2}{4!} + \cdots + \frac{x^{n-2}}{n!} + \cdots;$$

$$\frac{\sin x}{x} = 1 - \frac{x^2}{3!} + \frac{x^4}{5!} - \cdots;$$

$$\cos \sqrt{x} = 1 - \frac{x}{2!} + \frac{x^2}{4!} - \frac{x^3}{5!} + \cdots;$$

$$\frac{\sin \sqrt{x}}{\sqrt{x}} = 1 - \frac{x}{3!} + \frac{x^2}{5!} - \cdots;$$

$$\cosh x = \frac{e^x + e^{-x}}{2} = 1 + \frac{x^2}{2!} + \frac{x^4}{4!} + \frac{x^6}{6!} + \cdots;$$

$$\sinh x = \frac{e^x - e^{-x}}{2} = x + \frac{x^3}{3!} + \frac{x^5}{5!} + \cdots$$

etc.

In all these examples, the entire functions were elementary functions (exponential or trigonometric) or simple combinations of elementary functions.

But by no means can all entire functions be expressed as a finite combination of elementary functions. Such, for example, are the entire functions

$$f(x) = x + \frac{x^2}{2^2} + \frac{x^3}{3^3} + \ldots + \frac{x^n}{n^n} + \ldots ,$$

$$g(x) = \frac{x^2}{(\ln 2)^2} + \frac{x^3}{(\ln 3)^3} + \ldots + \frac{x^n}{(\ln n)^n} + \cdot$$

$$h(x) = x + \frac{x^2}{2^4} + \frac{x^3}{3^6} + \ldots + \frac{x^n}{n^{2n}} + \ldots$$

and infinitely many others, defined by series of the form (1) subject only to condition (3) imposed on their coefficients.

3. Up to now, we have considered entire functions, tacitly assuming that the coefficients in the power series representing them are real numbers and that the variable x also assumes real values. However, there is nothing to keep either the coefficients or the variable itself from being arbitrary complex numbers provided only the coefficients satisfy condition (3) as before. In fact, this condition ensures absolute convergence of the series for arbitrary values of the complex number x. In what follows, to avoid confusion, we shall use the letter x only to denote a real number and we shall denote a complex independent variable with the letter z, setting $z = x + iy$, where x and y are real numbers and $i = \sqrt{-1}$. As usual, the complex variable z will be represented geometrically by the point in the complex plane with coordinates x and y. In particular, for $y = 0$, the variable z assumes real values $z = x$. Any entire function can be regarded as a function of the complex variable z defined in the entire complex plane. Keeping the same terminology and notations for the exponential and trigonometric functions, we have

$$e^z = 1 + \frac{z}{1!} + \frac{z^2}{2!} + \frac{z^3}{3!} + \frac{z^4}{4!} + \ldots + \frac{z^n}{n!} + \ldots , \tag{7}$$

$$\cos z = 1 - \frac{z^2}{2!} + \frac{z^4}{4!} - \frac{z^6}{6!} + \ldots + (-1)^n \frac{z^{2n}}{(2n)!} + \ldots , \tag{8}$$

$$\sin z = z - \frac{z^3}{3!} + \frac{z^5}{5!} - \ldots + (-1)^{n-1} \frac{z^{2n-1}}{(2n-1)!} + \ldots . \tag{9}$$

4. Entire functions constitute a particular case of analytic functions of a complex variable. If to every point z in a region G in the complex plane, we assign one and only one complex number w, this means that we define in the region G a function of the complex variable z. Here, w is called the value of the function at the point z, and we write $w = f(z)$. Instead of f, we may use other letters of the Roman or Greek alphabet.

A function of a complex variable is said to be analytic in a domain G if, for every point z_0 belonging to G, there exists a neighborhood (that is, a disk with center at that point) in which the values of the function can be represented in the form of the limit of a series of powers of $z - z_0$:

$$w = f(z) = c_0 + c_1(z - z_0) + c_2(z - z_0)^2 + \ldots + \\ + c_n(z - z_0)^n + \ldots . \quad (10)$$

In the special case in which the domain G is an open disk with center at a point z_0, a sufficient condition for $f(z)$ to be analytic in the domain G is that the series (10) represent $f(z)$ throughout that disk.

To obtain the expansion of $f(z)$ in a power series in a neighborhood of any other point z_1 in the disk, we need only represent $z - z_0$ in the form

$$z - z_0 = (z - z_1) - (z_0 - z_1),$$

substitute this expression into (10), expand the powers $(z - z_0)^n$ by the binomial theorem so that each term becomes a polynomial in $z - z_1$, and then collect terms of like powers of $z - z_1$.

What was said above for a circular disk remains valid when G is the entire complex plane. We can regard this plane as a disk of infinite radius with center at any point, for example, at the coordinate origin.

In this case, we may set $z_0 = 0$ in formula (10) and require that the series converge everywhere in the plane (that is, that it be an everywhere-convergent power series, as we said above).

Thus, an entire function $f(z)$ can be defined as a function of a complex variable that is analytic in the entire plane of the complex variable z.

5. The *derivative* of a function $f(z)$ of a complex variable z at a point z_0 in the domain of definition of the function is defined as the limit (if it exists) of the ratio

$$\frac{f(z_1) - f(z)}{z_1 - z}$$

as $z_1 \to z$ (where $z_1 \neq z$):

$$f'(z) = \lim_{z_1 \to z} \frac{f(z_1) - f(z)}{z_1 - z}.$$

From this definition of a derivative, it follows that the differentiation rules established for functions of a real variable remain valid for functions of a complex variable. In particular,

$$[(z-z_0)^n]' = n(z-z_0)^{n-1}.$$

We can show that the function representing the limit of the power series (10) which converges in some disk with center at z_0 possesses derivatives of all orders everywhere in that disk. Each of these derivatives is obtained by termwise differentiation of (10) carried out the proper number of times:

$$f'(z) = c_1 + 2c_2(z-z_0) + 3c_3(z-z_0)^2 + \ldots + \\ + nc_n(z-z_0)^{n-1} + \ldots,$$

$$f''(z) = 1 \cdot 2c_2 + 2 \cdot 3c_3(z-z_0) + \ldots \\ \ldots + (n-1)nc_n(z-z_0)^{n-2} + \ldots,$$

$$f'''(z) = 1 \cdot 2 \cdot 3c_3 + 2 \cdot 3 \cdot 4c_4(z-z_0) + \ldots \\ \ldots + (n-2)(n-1)nc_n(z-z_0)^{n-3} + \ldots,$$

. . . .

Thus, from formulas (7)-(9), we obtain by successive differentiation

$$(e^z)' = e^z, \qquad (\cos z)' = -\sin z, \qquad (\sin z)' = \cos z.$$

If we set $z = z_0$ in the series for $f(z), f'(z), f''(z), \ldots, f^{(p)}(z), \ldots$, we obtain

$$c_0 = f(z_0), \quad c_1 = f'(z_0), \quad c_2 = \frac{f''(z_0)}{2!}, \ldots, \quad c_p = \frac{f^{(p)}(z_0)}{p!}, \ldots$$

Therefore, the coefficients of a power series are expressed by the values of the derivatives of the function represented by the series at the point z_0. Therefore, the series representing the function $f(z)$ can be written in the form

$$f(z) = f(z_0) + \frac{f'(z_0)}{1!}(z-z_0) + \frac{f''(z_0)}{2!}(z-z_0)^2 + \ldots \\ \ldots + \frac{f^{(p)}(z_0)}{p!}(z-z_0)^p + \ldots.$$

A series of this form is called the Taylor series of the function $f(z)$. Thus, a power series representing an analytic function $f(z)$ is the Taylor series for that function.

From the expressions that we have obtained for the coefficients of a power series, it follows that *if the functions* *representing two series of powers of $z - z_0$ coincide in some circle with center at z_0, the coefficients of like powers of $z - z_0$ must be equal.*

This is true because, if

$$a_0 + a_1(z - z_0) + \ldots + a_n(z - z_0)^n + \ldots =$$
$$= b_0 + b_1(z - z_0) + \ldots + b_n(z - z_0)^n + \ldots = f(z),$$

then,

$$a_n = \frac{f^{(n)}(z_0)}{n!} \quad \text{and} \quad b_n = \frac{f^{(n)}(z_0)}{n!},$$

that is, $a_n = b_n$ for $n = 0, 1, 2, 3, \ldots$. (We recall that the expression $f^{(0)}(z)$ denotes the function $f(z)$ itself and that 0! is taken as equal to 1.)

Since the function represented by a power series has a derivative, it follows that *a function $f(z)$ that is analytic in a domain G possesses a derivative at every point in that domain; that is, it is differentiable in the domain G. Therefore, it is continuous in G.*

It is remarkable that the converse theorem also holds: *If a function $f(z)$ of a complex variable z is differentiable in a domain G, it is analytic in that domain.*

For this reason, the definition of an analytic function of a complex variable can be represented in the following form: a function $f(z)$ of a complex variable z that is defined in a domain G is said to be analytic in that domain if it is differentiable in it. This is the definition that usually appears in textbooks on function theory.

Consequently, *an entire function can be defined as a function that is differentiable in the entire complex plane.*

Let $f(z)$ and $g(z)$ denote arbitrary entire functions. Then, from the rules of differentiation, we have

$$[f(z) \pm g(z)]' = f'(z) \pm g'(z),$$
$$[f(z) \cdot g(z)]' = f'(z) g(z) + f(z) g'(z),$$
$$\left[\frac{f(z)}{g(z)}\right]' = \frac{f'(z) g(z) - g'(z) f(z)}{[g(z)]^2} \qquad \text{(if } g(z) \neq 0\text{),}$$
$$\{f[g(z)]\}' = f'[g(z)] g'(z).$$

From the first two formulas, it follows that *the sum, difference, and product of entire functions are entire functions.*

It follows from the third formula that *the quotient of two entire functions is an entire function provided the denominator does not vanish anywhere.*

From the fourth, which represents the chain rule for differentiating a composite function, it follows that an *entire function of an entire function is an entire function.*

For example, the following are entire functions:

$$e^{\sin z},\ e^{e^z},\ \sin(e^z),\ \sin(\cos z).$$

6. Since power series converge absolutely in their circle of convergence, they possess many properties of finite sums.

In all cases, the operations of addition, subtraction, and multiplication are carried out on them according to the rules governing the same operations on polynomials arranged in increasing powers of z. Thus, if

$$f(z) = a_0 + a_1 z + a_2 z^2 + \ldots + a_n z^n + \ldots ,$$
$$g(z) = b_0 + b_1 z + b_2 z^2 + \ldots + b_n z^n + \ldots ,$$

then

$$\left.\begin{aligned}
f(z) \pm g(z) &= a_0 \pm b_0 + (a_1 \pm b_1) z + (a_2 \pm b_2) z^2 + \\
&\quad + \ldots + (a_n \pm b_n) z^n + \ldots , \\
f(z) g(z) &= a_0 b_0 + (a_0 b_1 + a_1 b_0) z + \\
&\quad + (a_0 b_2 + a_1 b_1 + a_2 b_0) z^2 + \ldots + \\
&\quad + (a_0 b_n + a_1 b_{n-1} + a_2 b_{n-2} + \ldots + a_n b_0) z^n + \ldots
\end{aligned}\right\} \quad (11)$$

If we know also that $g(z)$ does not vanish for any value of z, we may assert (cf. Section 5) that the quotient $f(z)/g(z)$ is an entire function. The power series representing it can be obtained by dividing the series for $f(z)$ by the series for $g(z)$ according to the rules for dividing polynomials arranged in increasing powers.

If we write

$$\frac{f(z)}{g(z)} = c_0 + c_1 z + c_2 z^2 + \ldots + c_n z^n + \ldots , \quad (12)$$

then using the last formula in (11) we may assert that every coefficient c_n is expressed in terms of the preceding quotients $c_0, c_1, \ldots, c_{n-1}$ according to the formula

$$c_n = -\frac{c_0 b_n + c_1 b_{n-1} + \ldots + c_{n-1} b_1}{b_0}. \quad (13)$$

7. Let us turn to the entire functions (7), (8) and (9). In formula (7), let us set $z = iw$, where w is again a complex variable. We find

$$e^{iw} = 1 + \frac{iw}{1!} - \frac{w^2}{2!} - \frac{iw^3}{3!} + \frac{w^4}{4!} + \cdots =$$
$$= \left(1 - \frac{w^2}{2!} + \frac{w^4}{4!} - \cdots\right) + i\left(w - \frac{w^3}{3!} + \frac{w^5}{5!} - \cdots\right),$$

so that by comparing these expressions with formulas (8) and (9), we see that

$$e^{iw} = \cos w + i \sin w. \tag{14}$$

This is a famous formula due to Euler. It expresses the exponential function in terms of trigonometric functions. In formulas (8) and (9), we note that the expansion of/the cosine contains only even powers of the variable and that the expansion of the sine contains only odd powers. Therefore, even for complex values of the independent variable, the cosine is an even and the sine an odd function. Therefore, by replacing w with $-w$ in formula (14), we obtain

$$e^{-iw} = \cos w - i \sin w. \tag{15}$$

By adding and subtracting formulas (14) and (15), we obtain two other of Euler's formulas, expressing the cosine and sine respectively in terms of the exponential function:

$$\cos w = \frac{e^{iw} + e^{-iw}}{2}, \qquad \sin w = \frac{e^{iw} - e^{-iw}}{2i}. \tag{16}$$

It follows from Euler's formulas that the exponential and trigonometric functions of a complex variable are, so to speak, close cousins in the world of entire functions.

As an example of multiplication of series, let us take the product of the two series for e^{z_1} and e^{z_2}, where z_1 and z_2 are arbitrary complex numbers.

Since

$$e^{z_1} = 1 + \frac{z_1}{1!} + \frac{z_1^2}{2!} + \frac{z_1^3}{3!} + \cdots + \frac{z_1^n}{n!} + \cdots,$$

$$e^{z_2} = 1 + \frac{z_2}{1!} + \frac{z_2^2}{2!} + \frac{z_2^3}{3!} + \cdots + \frac{z_2^n}{n!} + \cdots,$$

we have

$$e^{z_1}e^{z_2} = 1 + \frac{1}{1!}(z_1 + z_2) + \frac{1}{2!}(z_1^2 + 2z_1z_2 + z_2^2) +$$
$$+ \frac{1}{3!}\left(z_1^3 + \frac{3!}{2!\,1!} z_1^2 z_2 + \frac{3!}{1!\,2!} z_1 z_2^2 + z_2^3\right) + \cdots$$
$$\cdots + \frac{1}{n!}\left(z_1^n + \frac{n!}{(n-1)!\,1!} z_1^{n-1} z_2 + \frac{n!}{(n-2)!\,2!} z_1^{n-2} z_2^2 + \cdots\right.$$
$$\cdots \left.+ \frac{n!}{1!\,(n-1)!} z_1 z_2^{n-1} + z_2^n\right) + \cdots = 1 + \frac{1}{1!}(z_1 + z_2) +$$
$$+ \frac{1}{2!}(z_1 + z_2)^2 + \frac{1}{3!}(z_1 + z_2)^3 + \cdots + \frac{1}{n!}(z_1 + z_2)^n + \cdots.$$

From this it follows that

$$e^{z_1}e^{z_2} = e^{z_1 + z_2}.$$ (17)

This is the so-called *addition theorem* for the exponential function. We see that when we multiply two values of this function, the exponents (the complex numbers z_1 and z_2) are added.

Let us take the special case of $z_1 = z$ and $z_2 = -z$ (for any z). We obtain

$$e^z \cdot e^{-z} = e^0 = 1.$$ (18)

Since the product of the numbers $e^z \cdot e^{-z}$ is, on the basis of this formula, nonzero, it follows, first of all, that the *exponential function e^z is always nonzero;* that is, the equation $e^z = 0$ has neither real nor imaginary roots. (We use the term imaginary for any complex number that is not real; for example, i and $1 - i$ are imaginary numbers.)

Equation (18) enables us to verify a special case of the fact that the quotient of two entire functions is an entire function if the divisor does not vanish anywhere (cf. Section 5). Obviously, the quotient $1/e^z$ satisfies this condition. From formula (18), it follows that

$$\frac{1}{e^z} = e^{-z} = 1 - \frac{z}{1!} + \frac{z^2}{2!} - \frac{z^3}{3!} + \frac{z^4}{4!} - \cdots.$$

This is indeed an entire function. (We replaced z with $-z$ in formula (7).)

In Section 9, we shall show that *every entire function $g(z)$ that does not vanish anywhere can be represented in the form $g(z) = e^{h(z)}$, where $h(z)$ is also an entire function.* Of course the quotient $f(z)/g(z)$ can be represented in the form of a product $f(z)e^{-h(z)}$, from which we again see that this is an entire function (being the product of two entire functions).

If we multiply Eqs. (14) and (15), we obtain

$$e^{iw} \cdot e^{-iw} = (\cos w + i \sin w)(\cos w - i \sin w),$$

or, by virtue of Eq. (18),

$$1 = \cos^2 w + \sin^2 w.$$ (19)

Thus, the sum of the squares of the cosine and sine of any complex number is equal to 1.

In Eq. (17), let z_1 be any complex number z and set $z_2 = 2\pi i$. Then, we have

$$e^z e^{2\pi i} = e^{z+2\pi i}.$$

But, from Euler's formula (14), we have

$$e^{2\pi i} = \cos 2\pi + i \sin 2\pi = 1.$$

Therefore,

$$e^z = e^{z+2\pi i}, \tag{20}$$

that is, *the exponential function is periodic with purely imaginary period* $2\pi i$.

Let us now evaluate the absolute value and the argument of the complex number e^z. From formula (17), we obtain

$$e^z = e^{x+iy} = e^x e^{iy}.$$

But since $e^{iy} = \cos y + i \sin y$, we have

$$e^z = e^x (\cos y + i \sin y).$$

Thus, we have obtained a representation of e^z in trigonometric form: $r(\cos \varphi + i \sin \varphi)$. From this it follows that

$$|e^z| = e^x, \quad \mathrm{Arg}\,(e^z) = y + 2n\pi \quad (n = 0, \pm 1, \pm 2, \ldots).$$

The first of these formulas shows that, to evaluate the absolute value of e^z, we need to keep only the real part x in the exponent (and discard the iy). For example,

$$|e^{1+i\sqrt{2}}| = e.$$

8. Consider the equation

$$e^z = A. \tag{21}$$

Since we know that, for $A = 0$, this equation has no roots at all, we may assume that $A \neq 0$. It follows from the equality of the complex numbers, e^z and A that their absolute values are equal and that their arguments differ only by integral multiples of 2π. However, we noted in Section 7, that if $z = x + iy$, the absolute value of e^z is e^x and one of the values of the argument of e^z is y.

Therefore, (21) implies

$$e^x = |A|, \quad y = \arg A + 2n\pi \quad (n = 0, \pm 1, \pm 2, \ldots).$$

Therefore, $x = \ln |A|$ and

$$z = x + iy = \ln|A| + i(\arg A + 2n\pi), \tag{22}$$
$$n = 0, \pm 1, \pm 2, \ldots$$

Thus, an arbitrary root of Eq. (21) must be included in formula (22). Conversely, every number of the form (22) (and there are infinitely many of them) is a root of this equation. Specifically,

$$e^z = e^{\ln|A| + i(\arg A + 2n\pi)} = e^{\ln|A|} e^{i(\arg A + 2n\pi)} =$$
$$= |A|[\cos(\arg A + 2n\pi) + i\sin(\arg A + 2n\pi)] =$$
$$= |A|[\cos(\arg A) + i\sin(\arg A)] = A.$$

Thus, we have shown that, for every A with the single exception of zero, Eq. (21) has infinitely many roots (22). In other words, the *power-series equation*

$$1 + \frac{z}{1!} + \frac{z^2}{2!} + \cdots + \frac{z^n}{n!} + \cdots = A$$

has *infinitely many roots for an arbitrary nonzero complex number* A.

It is natural to call every root of Eq. (21) a value of the (natural) logarithm of the complex number A. Denoting in general by Ln A the power to which we need to raise e in order to obtain A, we rewrite formula (22) in the form

$$\text{Ln } A = \ln|A| + i\,\text{Arg } A = \ln|A| + i(\arg A + 2n\pi), \tag{22'}$$

where $n = 0, \pm 1, \pm 2, \ldots$.

From this it follows that the logarithm of an arbitrary nonzero complex number has infinitely many values, differing from each other by integral multiples of $2\pi i$. For $n = 0$, formula (22') yields the so-called *principal value* of the logarithm:

$$\ln A = \ln|A| + i\arg A. \tag{22''}$$

9. Let us regard the complex number A in Eq. (21) as an independent variable and let us treat the value of z corresponding to it, that is, the root of the equation, as a function of

A. This function $z = \operatorname{Ln} A$ is the inverse of the exponential function $A = e^z$. We saw in Section 8 that Ln A is a multiple-valued function defined in the entire complex plane except for the point $A = 0$ by formula $(22')$.

From the formula for differentiating the inverse of a function (which remains in force in the same form for functions of a complex variable), it follows that the derivative $(\operatorname{Ln} A)'$ exists and is equal to

$$\frac{1}{(e^z)'} = \frac{1}{e^z} = \frac{1}{A} \qquad (A \neq 0).$$

Instead of A, we shall use the conventional notation for an independent complex variable, which is z. We then have

$$\operatorname{Ln} z = \ln |z| + i \operatorname{Arg} z,$$
$$(\operatorname{Ln} z)' = \frac{1}{z} \qquad (z \neq 0).$$

The function Ln z is not an entire function, in the first place because it is not defined at $z = 0$ (where it becomes infinite) and, in the second place, because it is multiple-valued (as we saw, it has infinitely many values, differing from each other by integral multiples of $2\pi i$).

However, if $g(z)$ is any entire function that does not vanish at any point in the complex plane, then $f(z) = \operatorname{Ln} g(z)$ is also an entire function. More precisely, Ln $g(z)$ represents an infinite set of entire functions that differ from each other by constant values that are integral multiples of $2\pi i$. This is true because, by the general rule for differentiating a function of a function, we obtain

$$[\operatorname{Ln} g(z)]' = \frac{1}{g(z)} g'(z) = \frac{g'(z)}{g(z)},$$

that is, the functions Ln $g(z)$ possess derivatives at every point of the complex plane (remember that we are assuming that $g(z) \neq 0$) and hence are entire functions. As an example, we set $g(z) = e^z$. Then,

$$\operatorname{Ln}(e^z) = \ln |e^z| + i \operatorname{Arg} e^z;$$

But $|e^z| = e^x$ and $\operatorname{Arg} e^z = y + 2n\pi$ (cf. Section 5). Therefore,

$$\operatorname{Ln}(e^z) = \ln(e^x) + i(y + 2n\pi) = x + iy + i \cdot 2n\pi = z + 2\pi n i.$$
$$n = 0, \pm 1, \pm 2, \pm 3, \ldots$$

We see that $\mathrm{Ln}(e^z)$ represents an infinite set of entire functions

$$z, \; z+2\pi i, \; z-2\pi i, \; z+4\pi i, \; z-4\pi i, \; \ldots$$

From the above, we have the theorem (which we shall have frequent occasion to use): *If $f(z)$ is an entire function that does not vanish at any point, it can be represented in the form*

$$f(z)=e^{g(z)},$$

where $g(z)$ is an entire function.

Proof: From what was shown above, $\mathrm{Ln}\, f(z)$ represents an infinite set of entire functions that differ from each other by integral multiples of $2\pi i$. Let us denote any one of these by $g(z)$. Then,

$$\mathrm{Ln}\, f(z)=g(z)+2n\pi i \qquad (n=0,\pm 1,\pm 2,\ldots)$$

and, consequently,

$$f(z)=e^{\mathrm{Ln}f(z)}=e^{g(z)+2n\pi i}=e^{g(z)}.$$

Here, we used the fact that $2\pi i$ is the period of the exponential function (cf. Section 7). This completes the proof of the theorem.

_____

CHAPTER 2

The Maximum Absolute Value and
the Order of an Entire
Function

10. It is a remarkable fact that the coefficients of the power series representing a given entire function can be expressed in the form of integrals the integrands of which contain the given entire function.

Suppose that z describes the circle in the complex plane of radius $r > 0$ with center at the coordinate origin. Obviously, such a circle is represented by the equation $|z| = r$. Therefore, z can be represented in the form

$$z = r(\cos \varphi + i \sin \varphi).$$

The argument φ of the complex number z varies from 0 to 2π as z moves around the circle once in the counterclockwise direction.

Let $w = F(z)$ be an analytic function of the complex variable z that is defined in a domain containing the circle $|z| = r$. Then, at points on the circle, $F(z)$ can be regarded as a function of the single real variable φ: to every φ in $[0, 2\pi]$, there corresponds a definite z, and, consequently, the complex number

$$w = u + iv = F(z),$$

where u and v are the real and imaginary parts of w, is a function of φ. Therefore, u and v are functions of φ, which we denote by

$$u = P(\varphi), \quad v = Q(\varphi),$$

so that

$$F(z) = P(\varphi) + iQ(\varphi).$$

For every partition of the interval $[0,\ 2\pi]$ into subintervals defined by the numbers

$$\varphi_0 = 0 < \varphi_1 < \varphi_2 < \ldots < \varphi_{n-1} < \varphi_n = 2\pi,$$

let us construct an approximating sum for $F(z)$. To every value φ_k there corresponds a definite point z_k on our circle:

$$z_k = r(\cos \varphi_k + i \sin \varphi_k)$$

and one value of the function

$$F(z_k) = P(\varphi_k) + iQ(\varphi_k).$$

By definition, an approximating sum for the function $F(z)$, is an expression of the form

$$\sum_1^n F(z_k)(\varphi_k - \varphi_{k-1}) = \sum_1^n [P(\varphi_k) + iQ(\varphi_k)](\varphi_k - \varphi_{k-1}) =$$
$$= \sum_1^n P(\varphi_k)(\varphi_k - \varphi_{k-1}) + i \sum_1^n Q(\varphi_k)(\varphi_k - \varphi_{k-1}).$$

We note that the analytic function $F(z)$, being differentiable, is continuous. Therefore, we may conclude that its real and imaginary parts $P(\varphi)$ and $Q(\varphi)$ are also continuous on the interval $[0,\ 2\pi]$. As we make ever finer partitions of the interval $[0,\ 2\pi]$, so that the largest of the differences

$$\varphi_1 - \varphi_0,\ \varphi_2 - \varphi_1,\ \ldots,\ \varphi_n - \varphi_{n-1}$$

approaches 0, the sums

$$\sum_1^n P(\varphi_k)(\varphi_k - \varphi_{k-1}) \quad \text{and} \quad \sum_1^n Q(\varphi_k)(\varphi_k - \varphi_{k-1})$$

converge to limits, namely, to the integrals

$$\int_0^{2\pi} P(\varphi)\,d\varphi \quad \text{and} \quad \int_0^{2\pi} Q(\varphi)\,d\varphi,$$

respectively. Consequently, the complex-valued approximating sum

$$\sum_1^n F(z_k)(\varphi_k - \varphi_{k-1})$$

will also have a limit, which we denote by

$$\int_0^{2\pi} F(z)\, d\varphi.$$

From what we have said, it follows that

$$\int_0^{2\pi} F(z)\, d\varphi = \int_0^{2\pi} P(\varphi)\, d\varphi + i \int_0^{2\pi} Q(\varphi)\, d\varphi.$$

Thus, we have defined the integral of a complex function $F(z)$ in a particular case and we have expressed it in terms of integrals of the real and imaginary parts of that function. From the inequality

$$\left| \sum_1^n F(z_k)(\varphi_k - \varphi_{k-1}) \right| \leqslant \sum_1^n |F(z_k)|(\varphi_k - \varphi_{k-1}),$$

we obtain by taking the limit

$$\left| \int_0^{2\pi} F(z)\, d\varphi \right| \leqslant \int_0^{2\pi} |F(z)|\, d\varphi \, ;$$

that is, the absolute value of the integral of a function does not exceed the integral of the absolute value of that function.

Let us return to the problem of expressing an arbitrary coefficient a_p (for $p \geqslant 0$) in the power series representing an entire function in the form of an integral. To do this, we divide all terms of the series by z^p and integrate with respect to the variable φ from 0 to 2π. The division by z^p yields

$$\frac{f(z)}{z^p} = a_0 z^{-p} + a_1 z^{1-p} + \ldots + a_p + a_{p+1} z + \ldots ,$$

and the integration yields

$$\int_0^{2\pi} \frac{f(z)}{z^p}\, d\varphi = a_0 \int_0^{2\pi} z^{-p} d\varphi + a_1 \int_0^{2\pi} z^{-p+1} d\varphi + \ldots +$$

$$+ a_p \int_0^{2\pi} d\varphi + a_{p+1} \int_0^{2\pi} z\, d\varphi + \ldots ,$$

where $z = r(\cos\varphi + i \sin\varphi)$, the letter r denoting a constant.

We shall not stop here to prove the validity of term-by-term integration of the series. (Proof of this is reduced to proving that the series in the variable φ for fixed r converges uniformly).

On the right side, the integral with the coefficient a_p is equal to 2π, so that the corresponding term is equal to $2\pi a_{p^i}$. The integrand of each of the other integrals is a nonzero integral power of z. To see that all these integrals are equal to 0, note that if m is a natural number, then by de Moivre's formula

$$z^m = r^m (\cos m\varphi + i \sin m\varphi).$$

If $m = -k$ and $k > 0$, we have

$$z^m = \frac{1}{z^k} = \frac{1}{r^k (\cos k\varphi + i \sin k\varphi)} =$$
$$= r^{-k} [\cos(-k\varphi) + i \sin(-k\varphi)] = r^m (\cos m\varphi + i \sin m\varphi).$$

Thus, for any integer $m \neq 0$,

$$\int_0^{2\pi} z^m d\varphi = r^m \int_0^{2\pi} (\cos m\varphi + i \sin m\varphi) \, d\varphi =$$
$$= r^m \left[-\frac{\sin m\varphi}{m} + i \frac{\cos m\varphi}{m} \right]_0^{2\pi} = 0.$$

Therefore,

$$\int_0^{2\pi} \frac{f(z)}{z^p} \, d\varphi = 2\pi a_p,$$

so that

$$a_p = \frac{1}{2\pi} \int_0^{2\pi} \frac{f(z)}{z^p} d\varphi, \quad \text{where} \quad z = r(\cos\varphi + i \sin\varphi). \tag{23}$$

This formula is valid for $p = 0, 1, 2, 3, \ldots$. We denote by $M(r)$ the maximum absolute value of the function $f(z)$ in the closed disk* of radius r,

$$M(r) = \max_{|z| \leq r} |f(z)|^*).$$

---

*In the Appendix (Section 1), it is shown that the absolute value of an entire function attains its maximum over a closed disk not at an interior point of the disk but on the circle serving as its boundary. Therefore, the maximum absolute value of an entire function over a closed disk coincides with the maximum absolute value of that function over its boundary.

From formula (23), it follows that

$$|a_p| = \left| \frac{1}{2\pi} \int_0^{2\pi} \frac{f(z)}{z^p} \, d\varphi \right| \leqslant \frac{1}{2\pi} \int_0^{2\pi} \frac{|f(z)|}{|z|^p} \, d\varphi.$$

But, for $z = r(\cos \varphi + i \sin \varphi)$,

$$|z| = r \quad \text{and} \quad |f(z)| \leqslant M(r).$$

Therefore,

$$|a_p| \leqslant \frac{1}{2\pi} \int_0^{2\pi} \frac{M(r)}{r^p} \, d\varphi = \frac{M(r)}{r^p}, \quad p = 0, 1, 2, \ldots. \tag{24}$$

This is Cauchy's inequality for the coefficients of a power series.

11. The function $M(r)$ that we encountered in the preceding section plays an extremely important role in the theory of entire functions. Precise computation of it even for very simple entire functions can involve considerable difficulties. However, it is often sufficient to be able to find bounds for it from above and from below.

Let us consider first the case of a polynomial of degree n (where $n \geqslant 1$):

$$P(z) = a_0 + a_1 z + \ldots + a_n z^n, \quad a_n \neq 0.$$

If z lies on the circle of radius r with center at the coordinate origin, then $|z| \leqslant r$ and, consequently,

$$|P(z)| = |a_0 + a_1 z + \ldots + a_n z^n| \leqslant$$
$$\leqslant |a_0| + |a_1| |z| + \ldots + |a_n| |z^n| \leqslant |a_0| + \ldots + |a_n| r^n$$

or

$$|P(z)| \leqslant |a_n| r^n \left[1 + \left(\frac{|a_{n-1}|}{|a_n|} \frac{1}{r} + \ldots + \frac{|a_0|}{|a_n|} \frac{1}{r^n} \right) \right].$$

As $r \to \infty$, the sum in the parentheses approaches 0. Therefore, for any positive number $\varepsilon < 1$, there exists an $r_0(\varepsilon)$ such that, for $r > r_0(\varepsilon)$,

$$\frac{|a_{n-1}|}{|a_n|} \frac{1}{r} + \ldots + \frac{|a_0|}{|a_n|} \frac{1}{r^n} < \varepsilon. \tag{25}$$

Therefore, for $r > r_0(\varepsilon)$ and $|z| \leqslant r$,

$$|P(z)| \leqslant |a_n| r^n (1 + \varepsilon). \tag{26}$$

Consider the value of $|P(z)|$ at an arbitrary point z_0 on the circle $|z| = r$. We have $|z_0| = r$. At that point, inequality (26) is also satisfied (for $r > r_0(\varepsilon)$). On the other hand,

$$
\begin{aligned}
|P(z_0)| = |a_n z_0^n + (a_{n-1} z_0^{n-1} + \ldots + a_0)| \geqslant |a_n z_0^n| - \\
- |a_{n-1} z_0^{n-1} + \ldots + a_0| \geqslant |a_n| |z_0|^n - |a_{n-1}| |z_0|^{n-1} - \\
- \ldots - |a_0| = |a_n| r^n - |a_{n-1}| r^{n-1} - \ldots - |a_0| = \\
= |a_n| r^n \left[1 - \left(\frac{|a_{n-1}|}{|a_n|} \frac{1}{r} + \ldots + \frac{|a_0|}{|a_n|} \frac{1}{r^n} \right) \right].
\end{aligned}
$$

For $r > r_0(\varepsilon)$, we obtain on the basis of (25)

$$|P(z_0)| \geqslant |a_n| r^n (1 - \varepsilon). \tag{27}$$

Thus, for arbitrary $\varepsilon > 0$ and for sufficiently large r, the absolute value of the polynomial $P(z)$ at the point z_0, where $|z_0| = r$, satisfies the inequalities

$$|a_n| r^n (1 - \varepsilon) \leqslant |P(z)| \leqslant |a_n| r^n (1 + \varepsilon). \tag{28}$$

We shall use this double inequality in the Appendix. We note that it is obviously valid for a zeroth-degree polynomial (that is, for $n = 0$). Returning to (26), we conclude that this inequality remains valid at that point in the disk $|z| \leqslant r$ at which $|P(z)|$ attains its maximum $M(r)$. Therefore,

$$M(r) \leqslant |a_n| r^n (1 + \varepsilon), \quad \text{if} \quad r > r_0(\varepsilon). \tag{29}$$

On the other hand, the value of $|P(z)|$ at a point z_0 on the circle $|z| = r$ cannot exceed $M(r)$. Therefore, from inequality (27), we conclude that

$$M(r) \geqslant |a_n| r^n (1 - \varepsilon), \quad \text{if} \quad r > r_0(\varepsilon). \tag{30}$$

It follows from (29) and (30) that, for $r > r_0(\varepsilon)$,

$$1 - \varepsilon \leqslant \frac{M(r)}{|a_n| r^n} \leqslant 1 + \varepsilon,$$

and, since ε here is arbitrarily small, we have

$$\lim_{n\to\infty}\ \frac{M(r)}{|a_n|\,r^n}=1. \tag{31}$$

This relation can be worded as follows: *The maximum absolute value of a polynomial of degree n is asymptotically equal to the absolute value of the highest-degree term of the polynomial* (remember that $|a_n|r^n=|a_n\,z^n|$, where $|z|=r$).

12. Let us find the function $M(r)$ for e^z, $\cos z$, and $\sin z$. In order not to get these mixed up, we use the notations

$$M(r;\ e^z),\qquad M(r;\ \cos z),\qquad M(r;\ \sin z).$$

The same reasoning is used for all three of these. It is based on a bound for the absolute value of the limit of a power series.

From the formula

$$e^z=1+\frac{z}{1!}+\frac{z^2}{2!}+\dots+\frac{z^n}{n!}+\dots$$

we conclude that

$$|e^z|=\left|1+\frac{z}{1!}+\frac{z^2}{2!}+\dots+\frac{z^n}{n!}+\dots\right|\leqslant$$
$$\leqslant 1+\frac{|z|}{1!}+\frac{|z|^2}{2!}+\dots+\frac{|z|^n}{n!}+\dots.$$

On the closed disk of radius r with center at the coordinate origin, we have $|z|\leqslant r$. Therefore,

$$|e^z|\leqslant 1+\frac{r}{1!}+\frac{r^2}{2!}+\dots+\frac{r^n}{n!}+\dots\quad\text{for}\quad|z|\leqslant r.$$

Thus, $|e^z|$ does not exceed e^r anywhere on the disk $|z|\leqslant r$. However, at a point $z=r$ on its boundary, $e^z=e^r$ and $|e^z|=e^r$. Therefore, the absolute value of the exponential attains its greatest value at such a point. Consequently,

$$M(r;\ e^z)=\max_{|z|\leqslant r}|e^z|=e^r. \tag{32}$$

Analogously, from the formula

$$\cos z=1-\frac{z^2}{2!}+\frac{z^4}{4!}-\frac{z^6}{6!}+\dots,$$

we conclude that

$$|\cos z|\leqslant 1+\frac{|z|^2}{2!}+\frac{|z|^4}{4!}+\frac{|z|^6}{6!}+\dots,$$

and hence

$$|\cos z| \leqslant 1 + \frac{r^2}{2!} + \frac{r^4}{4!} + \frac{r^6}{6!} + \cdots$$

in the disk of radius r. The limit of the series on the right side of the last inequality is equal to $\cosh r = e^r + e^{-r}/2$ (cf. formulas in Section 2).

Thus,

$$|\cos z| \leqslant \frac{e^r + e^{-r}}{2}, \quad \text{if} \quad |z| \leqslant r.$$

But, at the point $z = ir$ on the circle constituting the boundary of the disk,* we have

$$\cos z = \cos (ir) = \frac{e^{i(ir)} + e^{-i(ir)}}{2} = \frac{e^{-r} + e^r}{2} \; *).$$

Thus, $(e^r + e^{-r})/2$ coincides with the maximum absolute value of the cosine on the disk $|z| \leqslant r$; that is,

$$M(r; \cos z) = \max_{|z| \leqslant r} |\cos z| = \frac{e^r + e^{-r}}{2}. \tag{33}$$

Finally, from the formula

$$\sin z = z - \frac{z^3}{3!} + \frac{z^5}{5!} - \frac{z^7}{7!} + \cdots,$$

we conclude that

$$|\sin z| \leqslant |z| + \frac{|z|^3}{3!} + \frac{|z|^5}{5!} + \frac{|z|^7}{7!} + \cdots,$$

so that

$$|\sin z| \leqslant r + \frac{r^3}{3!} + \frac{r^5}{5!} + \frac{r^7}{7!} + \cdots$$

on the disk of radius r. The limit of the series on the right side of the last inequality is equal to $\sinh r = (e^r - e^{-r})/2$ (cf. formulas in Section 2).

Thus,

$$|\sin z| \leqslant \frac{e^r - e^{-r}}{2}, \quad \text{if} \quad |z| \leqslant r.$$

---

*We note that the function $\cos z$ assumes the same value at $z = -ir$ since the cosine is an even function.

But at the point $z = ir$ on the boundary circle, *

$$|\sin z| = |\sin(ir)| = \left|\frac{e^{i\,(ir)} - e^{-i\,(ir)}}{2i}\right| = \left|\frac{e^{-r} - e^r}{2}\right| = \frac{e^r - e^{-r}}{2}\ *).$$

Therefore, $(e^r - e^{-r})/2$ coincides with the maximum absolute value of the sine on the disk $|z| \leq r$, that is,

$$M(r;\ \sin z) = \max_{|z|\,\leq\, r} |\sin z| = \frac{e^r - e^{-r}}{2}. \tag{34}$$

13. It is easy to see that the maximum absolute value of an entire function $f(z)$ is always a nondecreasing function of the radius r. This is true because, if $r_1 > r$, the disk of radius r_1 with center at the coordinate origin contains the disk of radius r with the same center. Therefore, when we seek the maximum value of $|f(z)|$ in the larger circle, that is, when we seek the number $M(r_1)$, we need to consider all the values of the absolute value of the function $f(z)$ in the smaller disk $|z| \leq r$ (and among these the value $M(r)$ and also the values of $|f(z)|$ in the annulus $r < |z| \leq r_1$. This means that $M(r_1)$ may either be greater than $M(r)$ (if there are values of $|f(z)|$ in the annulus that exceed $M(r)$) or equal to $M(r)$ (if there are no such larger values in it). Thus,

$$M(r_1) \geq M(r), \quad \text{if} \quad r_1 > r > 0. \tag{35}$$

As an example, let us show directly that the maximum absolute values of the functions listed in the preceding section increase with increasing $|z|$. We have seen that

$$M(r;\ e^z) = e^r, \quad M(r;\ \cos z) = \frac{e^r + e^{-r}}{2}, \quad M(r;\ \sin z) = \frac{e^r - e^{-r}}{2}.$$

For the first of these, the increase is obvious since this is an exponential function with base exceeding 1. For the last, $(e^r - e^{-r})/2$, the increase follows from the fact that e^r increases and e^{-r} decreases as r increases so that the difference $e^r - e^{-r}$ increases. To see that the function $(e^r + e^{-r})/2$ also increases (for $r > 0$), we can, for example, evaluate its derivative. We obtain

$$\left(\frac{e^r + e^{-r}}{2}\right)' = \frac{e^r - e^{-r}}{2}.$$

---

* $|\sin z|$ assumes the same value at the point $z = -ir$ since $\sin z$ is an odd function.

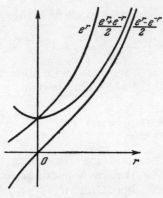

FIG. 1

Since it is positive for $r > 0$, the function $(e^r + e^{-r})/2$ does indeed increase for $r > 0$. Figure 1 shows the graphs of the three functions

$$e^r, \frac{e^r + e^{-r}}{2}, \quad \text{and} \quad \frac{e^r - e^{-r}}{2}.$$

14. Let us prove the following theorem of the nineteenth-century French mathematician Liouville:

If an entire function $f(z)$ is not identically constant, its maximum absolute value $M(r)$ approaches infinity as r increases without bound.

In each of the cases that we have considered above (namely, a polynomial of degree $n \geqslant 1$, the exponential function e^z, and the trigonometric functions $\cos z$ and $\sin z$), this theorem is obvious.

For example, in the case of a polynomial of degree $n \geqslant 1$, we saw that $\lim\limits_{r \to \infty} \dfrac{M(r)}{|a_n| r^n} = 1$ and hence $M(r)$ increases without bound with the same speed as does $|a_n| r^n$ (we recall that $a_n \neq 0$).

The functions

$$M(r; e^z), \quad M(r; \cos z), \quad M(r; \sin z).$$

also increase without bound. We note that

$$\lim_{r \to \infty} \frac{M(r; e^z)}{e^r} = 1, \quad \lim_{r \to \infty} \frac{M(r; \cos z)}{\frac{1}{2} e^r} = 1, \quad \lim_{r \to +\infty} \frac{M(r; \sin z)}{\frac{1}{2} e^r} = 1.$$

In other words, in each of these cases, $M[r; f(r)]$ increases with the speed of $\alpha \cdot e^r$ (where $\alpha = 1$ or $a = 1/2$) that is, infinitely faster than does an arbitrary power of r since $\lim\limits_{r \to +\infty} \frac{r^n}{e^r} = 0$, no matter how great n is. This last fact can be shown more easily if we represent e^r by its power series and discard all the terms except the one containing r^{n+1}. Specifically,

$$\frac{r^n}{e^r} = \frac{r^n}{1 + \frac{r}{1!} + \ldots + \frac{r^{n+1}}{(n+1)!} + \ldots} < \frac{r^n}{\frac{r^{n+1}}{(n+1)!}} =$$

$$= \frac{(n+1)!}{r} \to 0 \text{ as } r \to \infty.$$

Now, let us proceed to prove Liouville's theorem. Suppose that

$$f(z) = a_0 + a_1 z + \ldots + a_n z^n + \ldots . \tag{36}$$

On the basis of Cauchy's inequality (24),

$$|a_n| \leqslant \frac{M(r)}{r^n},$$

where $M(r)$ is the maximum absolute value of $f(z)$ in the disk $|z| \leqslant r$. Since $M(r)$ is a nondecreasing function of r (cf. Section 13), it will either remain bounded, that is,

$$M(r) \leqslant C, \text{ where } C > 0,$$

or approach ∞ as $r \to \infty$.

We prove the theorem by contradiction. Let us assume that this last fact is not true. Then,

$$|a_n| \leqslant \frac{C}{r^n} \text{ for all } r > 0 \text{ and } n = 0, 1, 2, 3, \ldots .$$

For every $n \geqslant 1$, the right side of this inequality approaches zero as $r \to \infty$. Since the left side of the inequality is independent of r, we have

$$|a_n| \leqslant 0, \text{ i.e., } a_n = 0 \text{ for } n \geqslant 1,$$

and this means that the power series (36) is reduced to the free term a_0; that is,

$$f(z) \equiv a_0.$$

We see that the assumption that $M(r)$ (and hence $|f(z)|$) is bounded leads to the conclusion that $f(z)$ is a constant. If this is not the case, then the function $M(r)$ cannot be bounded and, since it is nondecreasing, it approaches $+\infty$.

15. In the preceding section, we noted that the maximum absolute value of an nth-degree polynomial approaches ∞ with the speed of r^n (with some positive coefficient) and that the maximum absolute values of the functions e^z, $\cos z$, and $\sin z$ approach ∞ faster than does any power of r. These are special cases of the following theorem, which may be regarded as a generalization of Liouville's theorem:

If an entire function $f(z)$ is not a polynomial, its maximum absolute value increases faster than the maximum absolute value of any polynomial.

In other words, if we denote the maximum absolute value of a nonpolynomial entire function $f(z)$ by $M(r; f)$ and the maximum absolute value of a polynomial $P(z)$ by $M(r; P)$, we always have

$$\lim_{r \to \infty} \frac{M(r; P)}{M(r; f)} = 0. \tag{37}$$

Proof: Let us represent $f(z)$ by

$$f(z) = a_0 + a_1 z + \ldots + a_n z^n + \ldots . \tag{38}$$

Stating that $f(z)$ is not a polynomial means that the series (38) does not terminate with any n; that is, for every j, there exists an $n > j$ such that the coefficient of the term in z^n is nonzero. Let us denote the degree of the polynomial $P(z)$ by m and let us denote the coefficient of its leading term by b_m, assumed to be nonzero. Then, for fixed $\varepsilon_0 > 0$, we may assert that

$$M(r; P) \leqslant |b_m| r^m (1 + \varepsilon_0) \quad \text{for} \quad r > r_0 \tag{39}$$

(cf. inequality (29)). We shall also assume that $r > 1$.

From the terms of the series (36) with nonzero coefficients, let us choose a term of degree $p \geqslant m + 1$ (where $a_p \neq 0$). From Cauchy's inequality (24), we have

$$|a_p| \leqslant \frac{M(r; f)}{r^p}, \quad \text{where} \quad M(r; f) \geqslant |a_p| r^p \geqslant |a_p| r^{m+1}. \tag{40}$$

From (39) and (40), we conclude that, for $r > r_0$ and $r > 1$,

$$\frac{M(r; P)}{M(r; f)} \leqslant \frac{|b_m| r^m (1 + \varepsilon_0)}{|a_p| r^{m+1}} = \frac{|b_m| (1 + \varepsilon_0)}{|a_p| r}.$$

Therefore,

$$\lim_{r \to \infty} \frac{M(r;\, P)}{M(r;\, f)} = 0, \qquad (41)$$

which completes the proof. Since, for $|z| = r$,

$$|P(z)| \leqslant M(r;\, P),$$

we have

$$\frac{|P(z)|}{M(r;\, f)} \leqslant \frac{M(r;\, P)}{M(r;\, f)}.$$

From this and from (41), it follows that

$$\lim_{r \to \infty} \frac{|P(z)|}{M(r;\, f)} = 0 \qquad (|z| = r), \qquad (42)$$

for any polynomial $P(z)$.

16. Let us use the results of Section 15 to prove that the functions e^z, $\cos z$, $\sin z$, and other nonpolynomial entire functions are transcendental.

We recall that a function $f(z)$ is said to be *algebraic* if it satisfies identically an equation of the form

$$P_0(z) + P_1(z)f(z) + P_2(z)[f(z)]^2 + \ldots$$
$$\ldots + P_n(z)[f(z)]^n = 0, \qquad (43)$$

where P_0, P_1, ..., P_n are polynomials, where $n \geqslant 1$ and $P_n(z) \not\equiv 0$. That is, $P_n(z)$ is either a polynomial of degree no lower than the first or a nonzero constant.

Functions that are not algebraic (and here we are considering only analytic functions) are said to be *transcendental*. In other words, the statement that $f(z)$ is a transcendental function means that $f(z)$ does not satisfy identically any equation of the form (43) with coefficients subjected to the restrictions stated (that is, for all values of the complex variable z).

Let us prove the

Theorem. *If an entire function $f(z)$ is not a polynomial, it is transcendental.*

We prove this by contradiction. Suppose that $f(z)$ satisfies an equation of the form (43). Consider the sequence of disks of radius 1, 2, 3, ... with centers at the coordinate origin. In each disk of radius k (for $k = 1, 2, \ldots$), let z_k denote a point at which the function attains its maximum in that disk:

$$|f(z_k)| = M(k; f).$$

Since $\lim\limits_{k \to \infty} M(k; f) = \infty$ (by Liouville's theorem), the values of $|f(z_k)|$ increases without bound. Therefore, we may assume that $f(z_k) \neq 0$ at least for sufficiently large k. Furthermore, the absolute values $|z_k|$ also approach ∞. (Inside and on any circle of radius R, the absolute value of the function is bounded; therefore, the points z_k at which $|f(z_k)|$ exceeds the maximum of $|f(z_k)|$ inside and on that circle—which will be the case from some k on—must lie outside that circle). Let us now set $z = z_k$ in Eq. (43) and divide all terms by $[f(z_k)]$. We obtain

$$P_n(z_k) + \frac{P_{n-1}(z_k)}{f(z_k)} + \ldots + \frac{P_0(z_k)}{[f(z_k)]^a} = 0. \tag{44}$$

If $P_n(z_k)$ is a polynomial of degree at least equal to 1, it approaches ∞ as $k \to \infty$, and if it is a polynomial of degree 0, it is constant. But all the other terms on the left must approach 0 as a result of Eq. (42) of the preceding chapter. To see this, note that, for example,

$$\left| \frac{P_{n-1}(z_k)}{f(z_k)} \right| \leqslant \frac{M(k; P_{n-1})}{M(k; f)}$$

and, in general,

$$\left| \frac{P_{n-m}(z_k)}{[f(z_k)]^m} \right| \leqslant \frac{M(k; P_{n-m})}{M(k; f)} \cdot \frac{1}{[M(k; f)]^{m-1}} \qquad (m \geqslant 1).$$

On the basis of (42), all these quantities approach 0 (we recall that $M(k; f) \to \infty$). We thus have a contradiction: in Eq. (44), the term $P_n(z_k)$ cannot approach 0, whereas we have just shown that it and all the other terms must approach 0. This contradiction proves the theorem. In particular, we may assert that e^z, $\cos z$, and $\sin z$, are transcendental functions.

17. From what we have said, it follows that we may regard any entire transcendental function $f(z)$ as a sort of "polynomial of infinitely high degree."

In the first place, in the series

$$f(z) = a_0 + a_1 z + a_2 z^2 + \ldots + a_n z^n + \ldots,$$

we encounter terms of arbitrarily high powers of z with nonzero coefficients. In the second place, the maximum absolute value $M(r; f)$ of such a function increases more rapidly than does the maximum absolute value of any polynomial no matter how high its degree. We shall return to this point of view later, at the moment, we only remark that all transcendental entire functions should not be lumped together, so to speak, since it has been discovered that the maximum absolute value of some such functions increases infinitely faster than does that of others.

As an example, let us compare the maximum absolute values of the functions e^z, e^{z^k} (where k is a natural number $\geqslant 2$), and e^{e^z}. For the first, the maximum absolute value is equal to e^r:

$$M(r; e^z) = e^r.$$

The second can be expanded in a power series simply by replacing z with z^k in the expansion for the exponential function (7). We obtain

$$e^{z^k} = 1 + \frac{z^k}{1!} + \frac{z^{2k}}{2!} + \dots + \frac{z^{nk}}{n!} + \dots,$$

so that

$$\left| e^{z^k} \right| \leqslant 1 + \frac{|z|^k}{1!} + \frac{|z|^{2k}}{2!} + \dots + \frac{|z|^{nk}}{n!} + \dots.$$

Therefore, in the disk $|z| \leqslant r$,

$$\left| e^{z^k} \right| \leqslant 1 + \frac{r^k}{1!} + \frac{r^{2k}}{2!} + \dots + \frac{r^{nk}}{n!} + \dots = e^{r^k}.$$

On the other hand, at the point $z = r$, the values of e^{z^k} and e^{r^k} coincide. It follows from this that e^{r^k} is the maximum absolute value of e^{z^k} on the disk $|z| \leqslant r$:

$$M(r; e^{z^k}) = e^{r^k}.$$

To evaluate e^{e^z}, we can replace z with e^z in the series (7). We obtain

$$e^{e^z} = 1 + \frac{e^z}{1!} + \frac{e^{2z}}{2!} + \frac{e^{3z}}{3!} + \dots + \frac{e^{nz}}{n!} + \dots.$$

This is not a power series although it can be replaced by a power series if we expand each of its terms in a power series in accordance with formula (7) and then collect terms of like powers of z, arranged in increasing order. Noting that $|e^z| \leqslant e^r$ in the disk $|z| \leqslant r$, we obtain

$$\left| e^{e^z} \right| \leqslant 1 + \frac{|e^z|}{1!} + \frac{|e^z|^2}{2!} + \cdots + \frac{|e^z|^n}{n!} + \cdots \leqslant$$

$$\leqslant 1 + \frac{e^r}{1!} + \cdots + \frac{e^{nr}}{n!} + \cdots = e^{e^r}.$$

On the other hand, at the point $z = r$, the values of e^{e^z} and e^{e^r} coincide. From this it follows that e^{e^r} is the maximum absolute value of the function e^{e^z} in the disk $|z| \leqslant r$:

$$M(r;\ e^{e^z}) = e^{e^r}.$$

As we would expect, all these functions $M(r;\ e^z)$, $M(r;\ e^{z^k})$, $M(r;\ e^{e^z})$ approach ∞ as $r \to \infty$ (according to Liouville's theorem). But they do so with different speeds. It is easy to see, for example, that

$$\lim_{r \to \infty} \frac{e^r}{e^{r^2}} = 0, \quad \lim_{r \to \infty} \frac{e^{r^2}}{e^{r^3}} = 0, \ \ldots, \quad \lim_{r \to \infty} \frac{e^{r^k}}{e^{r^{k+1}}} = 0, \ \ldots$$

$$\ldots, \quad \lim_{r \to \infty} \frac{e^{r^k}}{e^{e^r}} = 0$$

(whatever the value of the natural number k). It follows from this that in the sequence of transcendental entire functions

$$e^z, \ e^{z^2}, \ e^{z^3}, \ \ldots, \ e^{z^k}, \ e^{z^{k+1}}, \ \ldots$$

the maximum absolute value of each increases with a speed infinitely greater than that of the preceding one and that the maximum absolute value of the function e^{e^z} increases faster than any of them.

We now show how we can measure in terms of specific numbers the maximum absolute value of each of these functions (except the function e^{e^z}), using the rate of increase of $M(r;\ e^z) = e^r$ as a standard. With this in mind, let us first look at functions that increase at a slower rate, taking, to begin with, the maximum absolute values of their logarithms instead of the functions themselves.

We obtain the sequence

$$\ln M(r; e^z) = r, \qquad \ln M(r; e^{z^2}) = r^2, \ldots, \qquad \ln M(r; e^{z^k}) = r^k,$$
$$\ln M(r; e^{z^{k+1}}) = r^{k+1} \ldots.$$

But even here, each successive function increases with an infintely greater speed than does the preceding one. Therefore, we again take the logarithms and we obtain the sequence

$$\ln \ln M(r; e^z) = \ln r, \quad \ln \ln M(r; e^{z^2}) = 2\ln r, \ldots,$$
$$\ln \ln M(r; e^{z^k}) = k \ln r, \ldots.$$

Obviously, the ratios of these last functions are constant numbers. Let us consider the sequence of these ratios:

$$\frac{\ln \ln M(r; e^{z^2})}{\ln \ln M(r; e^z)} = 2,$$
$$\frac{\ln \ln M(r; e^{z^3})}{\ln \ln M(r; e^z)} = 3, \ldots, \quad \frac{\ln \ln M(r; e^{z^k})}{\ln \ln M(r; e^z)} = k, \ldots.$$

Accordingly, we say that the order of the function e^{z^2} is 2, that the order of the function e^{z^3} is 3, and, in general, that the order of the function e^{z^k} (for $k = 1, 2, 3, \ldots$) is k (it being understood that we mean in each case the order of the increase in the maximum absolute value of the function in question relative to that of the function e^z). The order of the function e^z itself (which we chose for our standard), as determined by this procedure, is of course 1.

In the case of the function e^{e^z}, we have

$$\frac{\ln \ln M(r; e^{e^z})}{\ln \ln M(r; e^z)} = \frac{\ln \ln (e^{e^r})}{\ln r} = \frac{r}{\ln r} \to \infty \quad \text{as} \quad r \to \infty.$$

Therefore, we say that the order of the function e^{e^z} is ∞. In general, the order ρ of an entire function $f(z)$ is defined as the *limit* (if it exists) *of the ratio of the logarithm of the logarithm of* $M(r; f)$ *to the logarithm of the logarithm of* $M(r; e^z)$ *as* $r \to \infty$:

$$\rho = \lim_{r \to \infty} \frac{\ln \ln M(r; f)}{\ln \ln M(r; e^z)} = \lim_{r \to \infty} \frac{\ln \ln M(r; f)}{\ln r}. \tag{45}$$

If the ratio $\dfrac{\ln \ln M(r;\,f)}{\ln r}$ has neither a finite nor an infinite limit as $r \to \infty$, we refer to the limit superior of this ratio* as the order of the entire function $f(z)$:

$$\rho = \varlimsup_{r \to \infty} \frac{\ln \ln M(r;\,f)}{\ln r}. \tag{45'}$$

18. Formula (45) makes it possible to show with the aid of formulas (33) and (34) that the order of each of the functions $\cos z$ and $\sin z$ is 1. We have

$$M(r;\,\cos z) = \frac{e^r + e^{-r}}{2} = e^r \cdot \frac{1 + e^{-2r}}{2}.$$

Obviously, $e^{-2r} \to 0$ as $r \to \infty$. Therefore, the fraction on the right approaches $1/2$ as $r \to \infty$. Furthermore, when we take the logarithm, we obtain

$$\ln M(r;\,\cos z) = r + \ln \frac{1 + e^{-2r}}{2} = r \left(1 + \frac{\ln \dfrac{1 + e^{-2r}}{2}}{r} \right),$$

where the expression in the parentheses approaches 1 as $r \to \infty$. If we again take the logarithm, we get

$$\ln \ln M(r;\,\cos z) = \ln r + \ln \ln \left(1 + \frac{\ln \dfrac{1 + e^{-2r}}{2}}{r} \right),$$

and the second term on the right approaches 0 as $r \to \infty$. Therefore,

---

*Let $\phi(r)$ denote an arbitrary real function defined on the interval $1 < r < \infty$. (In the present case, $\phi(r) = \dfrac{\ln \ln M(r;\,f)}{\ln r}$.) If $\lim\limits_{r \to \infty} \phi(r) = a$ exists (either finite or infinite), then, for an arbitrary sequence of functions $\{r_n\}$ that approaches ∞ as $n \to \infty$, we have $\lim\limits_{n \to \infty} \phi(r_n) = a$. But if $\lim\limits_{r \to \infty} \phi(r)$ does not exist, there will be at least two sequences $\{r_n'\}$ and $\{r_n''\}$ that approaches ∞ as $n \to \infty$ such that $\lim\limits_{r \to \infty} \phi(r_n') \neq \lim\limits_{n \to \infty} \phi(r_n'')$. Now, consider all possible sequences $\{r_n\}$ that approach ∞ as $n \to \infty$ which for $\{\phi(r_n)\}$ has a limit. It can be shown that out of all the possible limits that one may obtain in this manner there exists a greatest (which may be either finite or infinite). This greatest limit is called the **limit superior** of $\phi(r)$ as $r \to \infty$, and it is denoted by $\varlimsup \phi(r)$.

$$\lim_{r \to \infty} \frac{\ln \ln M(r;\ \cos z)}{\ln r} = \lim_{r \to \infty} \left[1 + \frac{\ln \left(1 + \frac{\ln \frac{1 + e^{-2r}}{2}}{r} \right)}{\ln r} \right] = 1.$$

This means that the order of cos z is 1. In an analogous way, we can show that the order of sin z is 1 by using formula (34).

In all the examples that we have considered, the order of the entire functions was either an integer or infinity. However, there exists entire functions of fractional orders. For example, consider the function $f(z) = \dfrac{e^{\sqrt{z}} + e^{-\sqrt{z}}}{2}$. This is an entire function since

$$e^{\sqrt{z}} = 1 + \frac{\sqrt{z}}{1!} + \frac{z}{2!} + \frac{z\sqrt{z}}{3!} + \frac{z^2}{4!} + \cdots,$$

$$e^{-\sqrt{z}} = 1 - \frac{\sqrt{z}}{1!} + \frac{z}{2!} - \frac{z\sqrt{z}}{3!} + \frac{z^2}{4!} - \cdots,$$

and our function is represented by the convergent power series

$$\frac{e^{\sqrt{z}} + e^{-\sqrt{z}}}{2} = 1 + \frac{z}{2!} + \frac{z^2}{4!} + \frac{z^3}{6!} + \cdots .$$

Reasoning as in Section 12, we find, with the aid of this series, that

$$M \left(r;\ \frac{e^{\sqrt{z}} + e^{-\sqrt{z}}}{2} \right) = \frac{e^{\sqrt{r}} + e^{-\sqrt{r}}}{2}.$$

The reader himself can now verify that the order of the entire function $\dfrac{e^{\sqrt{z}} + e^{-\sqrt{z}}}{2}$ is equal to 1/2.

Let p/q denote any nonintegral rational number reduced to its simplest form (in which case, $q \geqslant 2$) and let us show that it is possible to construct an example of an elementary entire function $\varphi(z)$ of order equal to p/q. We note first that the complex number

$$\varepsilon = \cos \frac{2\pi}{q} + i \sin \frac{2\pi}{q}$$

is one of the values of $\sqrt[q]{1}$ since $\varepsilon^q = \cos 2\pi + i \sin 2\pi = 1$. The reasoning $q-1$ values of $\sqrt[q]{1}$ can be obtained by raising ε to the powers $2, 3, \ldots, q$:

$$\varepsilon^2,\ \varepsilon^3,\ \ldots,\ \varepsilon^q = 1.$$

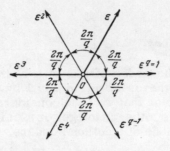

FIG. 2

Figure 2 shows all q values of $\sqrt[q]{1}$ graphically.
If m is an integral multiple of q, that is, if $m = nq$, then,

$$\varepsilon^m + \varepsilon^{2m} + \ldots + \varepsilon^{qm} = (\varepsilon^q)^n + (\varepsilon^q)^{2n} + \ldots + (\varepsilon^q)^{nq} = q. \tag{46}$$

On the other hand, if m is not a multiple of q, then

$$\varepsilon^m + \varepsilon^{2m} + \ldots + \varepsilon^{qm} = \frac{\varepsilon^m - \varepsilon^{qm}\varepsilon^m}{1 - \varepsilon^m} = 0, \tag{47}$$

since the numerator is now equal to 0 and the denominator is not. (Note that $\varepsilon^{qm} = 1$ and $\varepsilon^m = \cos\left(\dfrac{2\pi}{q}m\right) + i\,\sin\left(\dfrac{2\pi}{q}m\right)$ is different from 1 since m/q is not an integer.)

Consider now the following q series:

$$e^{\varepsilon\sqrt[q]{z^p}} = 1 + \frac{\varepsilon z^{\frac{p}{q}}}{1!} + \frac{\varepsilon^2 z^{2\frac{p}{q}}}{2!} + \ldots + \frac{\varepsilon^q z^p}{q!} + \frac{\varepsilon^{q+1} z^{(q+1)\frac{p}{q}}}{(q+1)!} + \ldots,$$

$$e^{\varepsilon^2\sqrt[q]{z^p}} = 1 + \frac{\varepsilon^2 z^{\frac{p}{q}}}{1!} + \frac{\varepsilon^{2\cdot 2} z^{2\frac{p}{q}}}{2!} + \ldots + \frac{\varepsilon^{q\cdot 2} z^p}{q!} + \frac{\varepsilon^{(q+1)2} z^{(q+1)\frac{p}{q}}}{(q+1)!} + \ldots,$$

$$\cdots\cdots\cdots\cdots\cdots\cdots\cdots\cdots\cdots\cdots\cdots\cdots\cdots\cdots\cdots\cdots$$

$$e^{\varepsilon^q\sqrt[q]{z^p}} = 1 + \frac{\varepsilon^q z^{\frac{p}{q}}}{1!} + \frac{\varepsilon^{q\cdot 2} z^{2\frac{p}{q}}}{2!} + \ldots + \frac{\varepsilon^{q\cdot q} z^p}{q!} + \frac{\varepsilon^{(q+1)q} z^{(q+1)\frac{p}{q}}}{(q+1)!} + \ldots.$$

Adding these equations, we obtain

$$e^{\varepsilon\sqrt[q]{z^p}} + e^{\varepsilon^2\sqrt[q]{z^p}} + \ldots + e^{\varepsilon^q\sqrt[q]{z^p}} = q + \frac{\varepsilon + \varepsilon^2 + \ldots + \varepsilon^q}{1!} z^{\frac{p}{q}} +$$

$$+ \frac{\varepsilon^2 + \varepsilon^{2\cdot 2} + \ldots + \varepsilon^{q\cdot 2}}{2!} z^{2\frac{p}{q}} + \ldots + \frac{\varepsilon^q + \varepsilon^{q\cdot 2} + \ldots + \varepsilon^{q\cdot q}}{q!} z^p +$$

$$+ \frac{\varepsilon^{q+1} + \varepsilon^{(q+1)2} + \ldots + \varepsilon^{(q+1)q}}{(q+1)!} z^{(q+1)\frac{p}{q}} + \ldots.$$

On the basis of formula (47), all the coefficients of the fractional powers vanish and, on the basis of formula (46), the numerator of each of the fractions serving as coefficient of an integral power of z is equal to q. Therefore,

$$e^{\varepsilon\sqrt[q]{z^p}} + e^{\varepsilon^2\sqrt[q]{z^p}} + \ldots + e^{\varepsilon^q\sqrt[q]{z^p}} = q + \frac{q}{q!}z^p + \frac{q}{(2q)!}z^{2p} + \frac{q}{(3q)!}z^{3p} + \ldots$$

If we divide both sides by q and denote the resulting entire function by $\varphi(z)$, we obtain*

$$\varphi(z) = \frac{e^{\varepsilon\sqrt[q]{z^p}} + e^{\varepsilon^2\sqrt[q]{z^p}} + \ldots + e^{\varepsilon^q\sqrt[q]{z^p}}}{q} =$$
$$= 1 + \frac{z^p}{q!} + \frac{z^{2p}}{(2q)!} + \frac{z^{3p}}{(3q)!} + \ldots * \big).$$

By using the same methods as in our previous examples, we see that

$$M(r;\varphi) = 1 + \frac{r^p}{q!} + \frac{r^{2p}}{(2q)!} + \frac{r^{3p}}{(3q)!} + \ldots = \frac{e^{\varepsilon r^{\frac{p}{q}}} + e^{\varepsilon^3 r^{\frac{p}{q}}} + \ldots + e^{\varepsilon^q r^{\frac{p}{q}}}}{q}.$$

Noting that $\varepsilon^q = 1$, we rewrite $M(r;\varphi)$ in the form

$$M(r;\varphi) = e^{r^{\frac{p}{q}}} \frac{1 + e^{(\varepsilon^{q-1}-1)r^{\frac{p}{q}}} + \ldots + e^{(\varepsilon^2-1)r^{\frac{p}{q}}} + e^{(\varepsilon-1)r^{\frac{p}{q}}}}{q}. \tag{48}$$

We may now proceed as when evaluating the order of $\cos z$ if we note that each of the terms of the form

$$e^{(\varepsilon^m - 1)r^{\frac{p}{q}}}, \qquad 1 \leqslant m \leqslant q-1,$$

approaches 0 as $r \to \infty$. To see this, let us evaluate the absolute value of each term. To do this, we need only keep thermal parts of the exponents (cf. end of Section 7). But, by de Moivre's formula

---

*We note that all the calculations with fractional exponents were necessary for z to appear raised to the fraction power p/q in the exponents of the e's in the center expression and for all powers of z in the right-hand expression to be integers (otherwise, the function itself would not be an entire function).

$$(\varepsilon^m - 1)\, r^{\frac{p}{q}} = \left[\left(\cos\frac{2\pi}{q} + i \sin\frac{2\pi}{q}\right)^m - 1\right] r^{\frac{p}{q}} =$$

$$= \left\{\left[\cos\left(m\,\frac{2\pi}{q}\right) - 1\right] + i \sin\left(m\,\frac{2\pi}{q}\right)\right\} r^{\frac{p}{q}} =$$

$$= \left[\cos\left(m\,\frac{2\pi}{q}\right) - 1\right] r^{\frac{p}{q}} + i \sin\left(m\,\frac{2\pi}{q}\right) r^{\frac{p}{q}}.$$

Therefore,

$$\left|e^{(\varepsilon^m - 1)\, r^{\frac{p}{q}}}\right| = e^{\left[\cos\left(m\frac{2\pi}{q}\right) - 1\right] r^{\frac{p}{q}}}. \tag{49}$$

Obviously, the difference $\cos\left(m\,\dfrac{2\pi}{q}\right) - 1$ is negative since $\cos\left(m\,\dfrac{2\pi}{q}\right)$, where $1 \leqslant m \leqslant q - 1$, is less than unity. Since $r^{\frac{p}{q}} \to \infty$ as $r \to \infty$, it follows that the expression (49) approaches 0 as $r \to \infty$, which means that $e^{(\varepsilon^m - 1)\, r^{\frac{p}{q}}}$ also approaches 0. Having shown this, we see that every fraction on the right-hand side of (48) approaches the limit $1/q \neq 0$. This makes it possible to carry out the remaining calculations as indicated at the beginning of this section. When these are all completed, we have

$$\lim_{r \to \infty} \frac{\ln \ln M(r; \varphi)}{\ln r} = \frac{p}{q}.$$

_____

CHAPTER 3

The Zeros of an Entire
Function

19. Let $f(z)$ denote a nonconstant entire function. A point a in the complex plane is called a *zero* of the function $f(z)$ if $f(a) = 0$. In other words, a zero of an entire function is a root of the equation

$$f(z) = 0.$$

If

$$f(z) = a_0 + a_1 z + a_2 z^2 + \ldots + a_n z^n + \ldots, \tag{50}$$

then, when we represent z in the form $z = a + (z - a)$ and expand z^n in powers of $z - a$, we have

$$z^n = [a + (z - a)]^n = a^n + \frac{n}{1} a^{n-1}(z - a) +$$

$$+ \frac{n(n-1)}{1 \cdot 2} a^{n-2}(z - a)^2 + \ldots + (z - a)^n.$$

Then, if we substitute this into (50) and collect terms of like powers of $z - a$, we obtain for $f(z)$ an everywhere-convergent series in powers of the difference $z - a$:

$$f(z) = c_0 + c_1(z - a) + c_2(z - a)^2 + \ldots + c_n(z - a)^n + \ldots. \tag{51}$$

As a useful exercise, we suggest that the reader carry out these calculations for the special case $f(z) = e^z$. He will obtain

37

$$e^z = e^a + \frac{e^a}{1!}(z-a) + \frac{e^a}{2!}(z-a)^2 + \ldots + \frac{e^a}{n!}(z-a)^n + \ldots .$$

Of course, this result can be represented in the form

$$e^z = e^a e^{z-a} = e^a \left[1 + \frac{z-a}{1!} + \frac{(z-a)^2}{2!} + \ldots + \frac{(z-a)^n}{n!} + \ldots \right].$$

If we set $z = a$ in (51) and note that, by hypothesis, $f(a) = 0$, we obtain

$$c_0 = 0.$$

Thus, if a is a zero of the function $f(z)$, the constant term in the expansion (51) is equal to zero. It may happen that the co-efficients of some of the terms following c_0 are also equal to zero (for example, we may have $c_1 = c_2 = 0$). However, it is impossible for all the coefficients in the series (51) to be equal to zero. (If they were, the function $f(z)$ would be identically equal to zero contrary to our hypothesis that $f(z)$ is not a constant.) Thus, in the series (51) there must exist a first nonzero coefficient c_k, where $k \geqslant 1$. The rank k of this coefficient, that is, the exponent in the expression $(z-a)^k$, is called the order of the zero in question.

Thus, if the order of a zero a of a function $f(z)$ is k, we have

$$f(z) = c_k(z-a)^k + c_{k+1}(z-a)^{k+1} + \ldots, \quad c_k \neq 0, \ k \geqslant 1. \qquad (52)$$

For example, let us take the function $\sin z$:

$$\sin z = z - \frac{z^3}{3!} + \frac{z^5}{5!} - \ldots .$$

From this expansion, we see immediately that the coordinate origin is a first-order zero of the function $\sin z$.

Let us now consider the function $z - \sin z$:

$$z - \sin z = \frac{z^3}{3!} - \frac{z^5}{5!} + \ldots .$$

Obviously, the coordinate origin is a third-order zero for this function.

20. If a is a zero of order k of an entire function $f(z)$, it follows from formula (52) that $f(z)$ can be represented in the form

$$f(z) = (z-a)^k [c_k + c_{k+1}(z-a) + \ldots], \tag{52'}$$

where $c_k \neq 0$ and $k \geqslant 1$. Since the series $(52')$ converges for all z, the series in the square brackets on the right side of $(52')$ converges for arbitrary z. (For $z = a$, the convergence is obvious; for $z \neq a$, the series is obtained by multiplying the convergent series (52) by the number $(z-a)^{-k}$.) Therefore, the limit of this last series is an entire function. We denote it by $\varphi(z)$:

$$\varphi(z) = c_k + c_{k+1}(z-a) + \ldots .$$

Since $\varphi(a) = c_k \neq 0$, the point a is not a zero of the function $\varphi(z)$. Thus, we obtain the

Theorem. If a is a zero of order k of an entire function $f(z)$, then $f(z)$ can be represented in the form

$$f(z) = (z-a)^k \varphi(z), \tag{53}$$

where $\varphi(z)$ is also an entire function of which the point $z = a$ is not a zero.

Let us note the case in which $f(z)$ is an nth-degree polynomial, where $n \geqslant 1$:

$$f(z) = a_0 + a_1 z + a_2 z^2 + \ldots + a_n z^n, \quad a_n \neq 0. \tag{50'}$$

In this case, when we expand the function in powers of $z - a$, as shown at the beginning of Section 19, we see that the highest power of $z - a$ in the expression for $f(z)$ is equal to n and that the coefficient of this power is equal to a_n:

$$f(z) = c_0 + c_1(z-a) + \ldots + c_n(z-a)^n, \quad c_n = a_n \neq 0. \tag{51'}$$

If a is a zero of $f(z)$ of order k (where $0 \leqslant k \leqslant n$), this formula takes the form

$$f(z) = c_k(z-a)^k + c_{k+1}(z-a)^{k+1} + \ldots + c_n(z-a)^n,$$

where $c_k \neq 0$ (for $1 \leqslant k \leqslant n$) and $c_n = a_n \neq 0$. Then,

$$f(z) = (z-a)^k [c_k + c_{k+1}(z-a) + \ldots + c_n(z-a)^{n-k}].$$

Comparison with the general formula (53) shows that, in the general case in which $f(z)$ is an nth-degree polynomial, the entire function $\varphi(z)$ is also a polynomial of degree $0 \leqslant n - k < n$. This polynomial does not vanish at $z = a$. The coefficient of the highest power of $z - a$ is a_n.

This result leads to a famous theorem of Bézout in the following form:

If $f(z)$ is a polynomial and $z = a$ is a kth-order zero of $f(z)$, then $(z - a)^k$ divides $f(z)$.

Let us return to the general case of an entire function $f(z)$ (which, as a special case, may be a polynomial).

Let $b \neq a$ denote an lth-order zero of the function $f(z)$. It follows from formula (53) that the point b will also be a zero of the function $\varphi(z)$ since

$$f(b) = (b - a)^k \varphi(b) = 0,$$

and the inequality $b - a \neq 0$ implies that $\varphi(b) = 0$.

Let us show that b is a zero of order l of the function $\varphi(z)$ also. Let us suppose that this is not the case and that the order l_1 of the point b as a zero of the function $\varphi(z)$ is not equal to l. For example, suppose that $l_1 < l$. Then, we have

$$f(z) = (z - b)^l \psi(z) \quad \text{and} \quad \varphi(z) = (z - b)^{l_1} \psi_1(z),$$

where $\psi(z)$ and $\psi_1(z)$ are entire functions for which the point b is not a zero. From formula (53), we conclude that

$$(z - b)^l \psi(z) = (z - a)^k (z - b)^{l_1} \psi_1(z).$$

From this, when we divide by $(z - b)^{l_1}$ (recall that, by our assumption, $l_1 < l$), we obtain

$$(z - b)^{l - l_1} \psi(z) = (z - a)^k \psi_1(z). \tag{53'}$$

Strictly speaking, we have proven this relationship only for $z \neq b$, but since the functions on both sides are continuous at $z = b$, it is also valid at $z = b$. If we set $z = b$, we obtain 0 on the left and the number $(b - a)^k \psi_1(b) \neq 0$ on the right. This contradiction proves that the assumption $l_1 < l$ is not valid. In just the same way, we can show that the assumption that $l_1 > l$ also leads to a contradiction. Thus, $l_1 = l$.

We have shown that every zero of the function $f(z)$ distinct from a is a zero of the same order of the function $\varphi(z)$. From formula (53), it also follows that every zero of $\varphi(z)$ must be a zero of $f(z)$. Therefore, the entire function $\varphi(z)$ in formula (53) has the same zeros—and of the same order—as does the function $f(z)$ except that the point a is not a zero of $\varphi(z)$.

If we apply the result that we have obtained to the function $\varphi(z)$ and to one of the zeros $b \neq a$ of order l of the function $f(z)$, we obtain

$$\varphi(z) = (z - b)^l \psi(z), \tag{54}$$

where $\psi(z)$ is an entire function possessing the same zeros as does the function $\varphi(z)$ (and of the same orders) except for the point b which is not a zero of $\psi(z)$. Consequently, the function $f(z)$ has the same zeros as does the function $\psi(z)$ except for the two points a and b.

It follows from formulas (53) and (54) that

$$f(z) = (z-a)^k (z-b)^l \psi(z). \tag{55}$$

Continuing this reasoning (it can be carried further by induction), we obtain the following result:

If $a, b, \ldots, c$ are distinct zeros of $f(z)$ with orders equal respectively to $k, l, \ldots, m$, then $f(z)$ can be represented in the form

$$f(z) = (z-a)^k (z-b)^l \ldots (z-c)^m \omega(z), \tag{56}$$

where $\omega(z)$ is an entire function possessing the same zeros as does $f(z)$ and of the same orders except that the points $a, b, \ldots, c$ are not zeros of $\omega(z)$.

Of exceptional importance is the case in which the points $a, b, \ldots, c$ constitute *all* the zeros of $f(z)$. This means that $f(z)$ has only finitely many zeros in the entire complex plane. Then, the entire function $\omega(z)$ vanishes nowhere and, from Section 9, can be represented in the form

$$\omega(z) = e^{g(z)},$$

where $g(z)$ is an entire function.

We obtain the following

Theorem. Suppose that an entire function $f(z)$ has only finitely many zeros $a, b, \ldots, c$ in the complex plane. Let $k, l, \ldots, m$ denote the orders of these zeros. Then, $f(z)$ can be represented in the form

$$f(z) = (z-a)^k (z-b)^l \ldots (r-e)^m e^{g(z)}, \tag{57}$$

where $g(z)$ is an entire function.

Noting that $(z-a)^k (z-b)^l \ldots (z-c)^m$ is a polynomial of degree $k+l+\ldots+m = n$, we conclude that every entire function possessing only finitely many zeros in the whole complex plane is equal to the product of some polynomial and a function of the form $e^{g(z)}$, where $g(z)$ is an entire function.

In the case in which the function $f(z)$ itself is a polynomial of degree n, the function $\omega(z)$ in formula (56) is also a polynomial.

If a, b, ..., c exhaust all the zeros of $f(z)$, then $\omega(z)$ is a polynomial possessing no zeros. From the fundamental theorem of algebra (which we shall prove in Section 22), it follows that $\omega(z)$ cannot be a polynomial of degree $\geqslant 1$, since any such polynomial has one or more zeros. Therefore, the degree of $\omega(z)$ is equal to zero; that is, $\omega(z)$ is a constant. From this it follows that the sum of the orders of all the zeros of $f(z)$ is equal to n:

$$k + l + \ldots + m = n$$

and that

$$\omega(z) \equiv a_n.$$

Therefore, the expansion (57) for a polynomial takes the familiar form

$$f(z) = a_n (z - a)^k (z - b)^l \ldots (z - c)^m.$$

21. In order to draw some conclusions regarding the zeros of an entire function in the case in which there are infinitely many of them, let us prove the following

Lemma. If $f(z)$ is an entire function not identically equal to zero, then, for every point z_0 in the plane, there exists a disk with center at that point in which $f(z)$ has no zeros except possibly the point z_0 itself.

Proof: Let us suppose first that $f(z_0) \neq 0$. Then, $|f(z_0)|$ is a positive number. Because of the continuity of the function $f(z)$ (its continuity being an automatic consequence of its differentiability) there exists for every $\varepsilon > 0$ a disk with center at z_0 in which

$$|f(z) - f(z_0)| < \varepsilon$$

and, in particular,

$$|f(z)| = |f(z_0) + [f(z) - f(z_0)]| \geqslant$$
$$\geqslant |f(z_0)| - |f(z) - f(z_0)| > |f(z_0)| - \varepsilon.$$

Let us take $\varepsilon = |f(z_0)|$. Then, in the corresponding disk,

$$|f(z)| > |f(z_0)| - |f(z_0)| = 0 \quad \text{or} \quad |f(z)| > 0.$$

Hence,

$$f(z) \neq 0.$$

Thus, in the case in which $f(z_0) \neq 0$, there exists a disk with center at z_0 containing no zero of the function.

Let us suppose now that $f(z_0) = 0$ and that k is the order of the zero z_0. Then (cf. Section 20),

$$f(z) = (z - z_0)^k \, \varphi(z),$$

where $\varphi(z)$ is an entire function that does not vanish at z_0. From what we have just proven, there exists a disk with center at z_0 in which $\varphi(z)$ does not vanish. Obviously, in that disk, $f(z)$ has no zeros other than z_0. This completes the proof of the lemma.

From this proposition, we derive the

Theorem. An entire function $f(z)$ not identically zero cannot have infinitely many zeros in any disk of finite radius.

Proof (by contradiction): Suppose that the function $f(z)$ has infinitely many zeros in the disk $|z| \leqslant r$. Then, in accordance with the familiar Bolzano–Weierstrass theorem (cf., for example, G. M. Fikhtengol'ts, *Osnovy matematicheskogo analiza* [Fundamentals of Mathematical Analysis], Vol. I, p. 239), somewhere on this disk there is a cluster point z_0 of the set of zeros of $f(z)$. This means that in an arbitrary disk with center at z_0 there are infinitely many zeros of the function $f(z)$, which contradicts the lemma which we have just proven.

As a corollary, we obtain the following *uniqueness theorem* for entire functions:

Theorem. If the values of two entire functions $f(z)$ and $g(z)$ coincide at infinitely many points belonging to some disk K of finite radius, these functions are identically equal:

$$f(z) \equiv g(z).$$

Proof: The difference $f(z) - g(z) = \varphi(z)$ is an entire function that vanishes at every point at which $f(z) = g(z)$. If we assume that $\varphi(z) \not\equiv 0$, we arrive at a contradiction with the theorem proven above. Therefore, $\varphi(z) \equiv 0$; that is, $f(z) \equiv g(z)$.

In particular, if the function $f(z)$ assumes a single value A at infinitely many points on a disk K, then $f(z) \equiv A$. To see this, we need only apply the theorem that we have just proven to $f(z)$, taking $g(z) \equiv A$.

Let us return to the case of a single entire function $f(z) \not\equiv 0$. Note that none of the above propositions keep this function from having an infinite set of zeros in the whole complex plane. For example, every integral multiple of π is a zero of the function $\sin z$:

$$n\pi, \quad n = 0, \pm 1, \pm 2, \ldots .$$

Let us suppose that $f(z)$ has infinitely many zeros in the complex plane and let us consider the disks of radius 1, 2, 3, ... with center at the coordinate origin. From what was said above, each of these disks contains only finitely many zeros of $f(z)$. This enables us to number *all* the zeros of $f(z)$ without omitting any and without repeating. Here is how this may be done. First, let us number in any order all the zeros in the disk $|z| \leqslant 1$. (For example, we could order them in order of increasing absolute value and zeros having the same absolute value could be ordered according to increasing argument.) Let us denote the lowest integer not used in the process by $k_1 \geqslant 1$. (Then, in the disk $|z| \leqslant 1$, there will be $k_1 - 1$ distinct zeros of the function.) We now proceed to number the zeros in the annulus between the two circles $|z| = 1$ and $|z| = 2$ (more precisely, in the annulus $1 < |z| \leqslant 2$), assigning to the first such the integer k_1. Let k_2 denote the lowest integer not used in doing so. Then, we turn to the annulus $2 < |z| \leqslant 3$ and proceed to number the zeros contained in it, beginning with the integer k_2. We repeat this process indefinitely. From this, it follows that when an entire function $f(z)$ has infinitely many zeros in the complex plane, all these zeros can be arranged in a sequence

$$z_1, \ z_2, \ z_3, \ldots, \ z_n, \ldots,$$

for example, with

$$|z_1| \leqslant |z_2| \leqslant \ldots \leqslant |z_n| \leqslant |z_{n+1}| \leqslant \ldots .$$

The limit of the sequence $\{z_n\}$ is ∞:

$$\lim_{n \to \infty} z_n = \infty.$$

CHAPTER 4 _____

The Fundamental Theorem
of Algebra and Picard's
Little Theorem

22. Liouville's theorem proven in Section 14 enables us to establish rather simply the so-called fundamental theorem of algebra:

The equation

$$a_0 + a_1 z + \ldots + a_n z^n = 0, \quad where \quad n \geqslant 1 \text{ and } a_n \neq 0, \qquad (58)$$

has at least one complex root.

Obviously, this theorem has to do with a general and extremely important property of polynomials of degree $n \geqslant 1$. If we set $P_n(z) = a_0 + a_1 z + \ldots + a_n z^n$, we can prove this theorem by contradiction. If the theorem is false, $P_n(z)$ does not vanish anywhere in the complex plane. Therefore, the function $f(z) = 1/P_n(z)$ is an entire function since it is the quotient of two entire functions (cf. Section 5). Obviously, it is not a constant since the denominator approaches ∞ as $z \to \infty$. (This follows, for example, from formula (27) as applied to an arbitrary point z_0 in the complex plane and to any polynomial of degree $n \geqslant 1$.) According to Liouville's theorem, the maximum absolute value of such a function $M(r; f)$ must approach ∞ as $r \to \infty$. But this contradicts the fact that the function itself approaches zero (since the denominator of the fraction $1/P(z)$ approaches ∞, and the numerator remains constant). This contradiction proves the theorem.

If we count each root of Eq. (58) a number of times corresponding to its multiplicity, we may now assert that the *number of all roots of Eq. (58) coincides with the degree of the polynomial* $f(z)$:

$$k + l + \ldots + m = n$$

(cf. end of Section 20).

23. In Section 17, we regarded the transcendental entire function

$$f(z) = a_0 + a_1 z + a_2 z^2 + \ldots + a_n z^n + \ldots \qquad (59)$$

as a sort of polynomial of infinitely high degree. We are now at a stage where we can check the soundness of that point of view. If the analogy is valid, the equation "of infinitely high degree"

$$a_0 + a_1 z + \ldots + a_n z^n + \ldots = 0 \qquad (60)$$

must have infinitely many roots. However, we are immediately disappointed in this. The equation

$$1 + \frac{z}{1!} + \frac{z^2}{2!} + \ldots + \frac{z^n}{n!} + \ldots = 0, \qquad (61)$$

which is simply the equation $e^z = 0$, does not have any root at all, as was shown in Section 7. But the situation can be saved by a slight though valuable compromise. Let us return to the case of a polynomial $P_n(z)$ of degree $n \geqslant 1$. Instead of Eq. (58) let us consider an equation of the more general form

$$a_0 + a_1 z + \ldots + a_n z^n = A, \qquad (58')$$

where A is an arbitrary complex number. Obviously, this equation also has n roots since it reduces to an equation of degree n of the type that we were just looking at:

$$Q_n(z) = 0, \quad \text{where} \quad Q_n(z) = P_n(z) - A.$$

Thus, Eq. (58') for arbitrary A has roots equal in number to the degree of the equation, namely, n.

Corresponding to the switch from (58) to (58'), let us consider not Eq. (61) but the more general equation

$$1 + \frac{z}{1!} + \frac{z^2}{2!} + \ldots + \frac{z^n}{n!} + \ldots = A \quad \text{or} \quad e^z = A, \qquad (61')$$

where A is any complex number.

In Section 8, it was shown that this equation has infinitely many zeros for arbitrary $A \neq 0$; that is, the number of its roots is again equal to the degree of the equation, namely, ∞. Consequently, the analogy between polynomials and entire transcendental functions (in the present case, e^z) is preserved for all A other than one exceptional value.

Instead of Eq. (61'), let us consider the equation

$$\cos z = A. \tag{62}$$

If we write $\cos z$ in exponential form in accordance with Euler's formula (16), we obtain

$$\frac{e^{iz} + e^{-iz}}{2} = A,$$

or, noting that $e^{-iz} = 1/e^{iz}$ and making some elementary manipulations with the equation, we have

$$e^{2iz} - 2Ae^{iz} + 1 = 0. \tag{63}$$

If we now set

$$e^{iz} = w, \tag{64}$$

the equation becomes the quadratic equation

$$w^2 - 2Aw + 1 = 0,$$

from which we get

$$w = A + \sqrt{A^2 - 1} = A + i\sqrt{1 - A^2}. \tag{65}$$

(We do not write the symbol $\pm$ in front of the radical, it being understood that both values of the square root must be considered.) To find the roots of Eq. (62), starting with w, we need to solve Eq. (64). We already know that this equation is satisfied by infinitely many values of the exponent iz (and, consequently, infinitely many values of z) provided $w \neq 0$, namely,

$$iz = \operatorname{Ln} w \text{ and } z = -i\operatorname{Ln} w = -i\operatorname{Ln}(A + i\sqrt{1 - A^2}). \tag{66}$$

But it follows from formula (65) that if $w = 0$, we have $i\sqrt{1 - A^2} = -A$, so that $A^2 - 1 = A^2$, which is impossible. Thus, for any A, the value of w determined by formula (65) is nonzero. Therefore, Eq. (64) and, consequently, Eq. (62) have infinitely many roots for arbitrary A (with no exception).

24. It turns out that the principles disclosed in the examples of the equations

$$e^z = A \quad \text{and} \quad \cos z = A,$$

hold for all transcendental entire functions. Specifically, in 1878, the French mathematician Picard proved the following remarkable proposition:

Picard's little theorem. If $f(z)$ is a transcendental entire function, then the equation

$$f(z) = A, \tag{67}$$

where A is any complex number, has infinitely many roots except possibly for one single value of A (which varies from function to function) for which the equation may have only finitely many roots or possibly no root at all.

For the function e^z, such an exceptional value is the value $A = 0$. For the function $\cos z$, there is no exceptional value. One can show in the same manner as for $\cos z$ that the function $\sin z$ also has no exceptional value, that is, that the equation

$$\sin z = A$$

has infinitely many roots regardless of the value of the complex number A.

Let us now see that sort of compromise we should seek in order to regain the right to regard transcendental entire functions as polynomials of infinitely high degree. This compromise consists in adding another possible exception to the general rule for the given function with the number of roots of Eq. (67) may not coincide with the "degree" of this equation (which is infinite).

Picard obtained various formulations that strengthen the preceding theorem and make it more precise. One of these is as follows:

If the order of $f(z)$ is an finite nonintegral number, then Eq. (67) has infinitely many roots for all values of A (with no exceptions).

Thus, in Section 18, it was noted that the order of the entire function $e^{\sqrt{z}} + e^{-\sqrt{z}}./2$ is equal to $1/2$. Therefore, we may assert that the equation

$$\frac{e^{\sqrt{z}} + e^{-\sqrt{z}}}{2} = A \tag{68}$$

has infinitely many roots for every complex number A. In the present case, we can see that this is true without referring to general theorems by reducing the equation to the case considered above, that is, reducing it to the equation $\cos z = A$. If we make the substitution

$$\sqrt{z} = i\zeta,$$

Eq. (68) then becomes

$$\frac{e^{i\zeta} + e^{-i\zeta}}{2} = A \quad \text{or} \quad \cos \zeta = A.$$

But this last equation has infinitely many roots for arbitrary A (see Section 23). To each of these roots ζ there corresponds the root $z = (i\zeta)^2 = -\zeta^2$ of Eq. (68).

25. Transcendental equations that are graphically solved in school courses include equations of the following types:

$$a^x = Ax, \quad a^x = Ax^2, \quad \sin x = Ax, \text{ etc.}$$

In all these examples, the left-hand member is a transcendental entire function and the right-hand member is a polynomial (here, either x or x^2) multiplied by some coefficient A. Thus, all of these are equations of the form

$$f(z) = AP(z), \tag{69}$$

where $f(z)$ is a transcendental entire function and $P(z)$ is a polynomial.

The theorems in Section 24 do not enable us to draw a conclusion as to the number of roots of Eq. (69) for a given number A. If we write this equation in the form

$$f(z) - AP(z) = 0,$$

we see that the problem consists in finding the zeros of the entire function $f(z) - AP(z)$. However, it may happen that the number on the right side of this equation is an exceptional value of the function $f(z) - AP(z)$, in which case Eq. (69) will have only finitely many roots.

The following theorem tells us what the situation is with regard to the number of roots of equations of the form (69):

If $f(z)$ is a transcendental entire function and $P(z)$ is a non-zero polynomial, then Eq. (69) has infinitely many roots for all values of A except possibly for a single exceptional value (this depending on $f(z)$ and $P(z)$).

The statement of Picard's little theorem given in the preceding section follows from this as a special case when $P(z) \equiv 1$. Therefore, if we can prove the theorem above, Picard's theorem will also be proven. Such a proof is given in the Appendix (Section 1), though under the assumption that the order of the function $f(z)$ is a finite number. There, we show that if the order of $f(z)$ is a fraction, there will be no exceptional value of A.

Let us apply the theorem as just stated to the special cases listed at the beginning of this section.

We note without loss of generality that we may take the base a (where $a \neq 1$) of the exponential function equal to e because, if $a \neq e$, we can, by setting $a = e^{\ln a}$, write the equation $a^x = Ax$ in the form $e^{x \ln a} = Ax$. If we then set $x_1 = x \ln a$, we have an equation in the new unknown x_1:

$$e^{x_1} = \frac{A}{\ln a} x_1 = A_1 x_1.$$

For example, the equation $2^x = 2x$ becomes $e^{x_1} = \frac{2}{\ln 2} x_1$.

Thus, let us look at the equation

$$e^z = Az. \tag{70}$$

Let us first assume that A is a real number and let us seek real roots of this equation. Using a graphical approach, we draw a line through the coordinate origin tangent to the curve $y = e^x$ (see Fig. 3). If (x_0, y_0) is the point of tangency, the equation for the tangent will be

$$y - y_0 = y_0' (x - x_0),$$

where $y_0 = e^{x_0}$ and $y_0' = \frac{de^x}{dx}\Big|_{x = x_0} = e^{x_0}$. Expressing the fact that the tangent passes through the coordinate origin $(0, 0)$, we have

$$-y_0 = -y_0' x_0, \text{ i.e., } e^{x_0} = e^{x_0} x_0, \text{ or } x_0 = 1, y_0 = e^{x_0} = e;$$

that is, the slope of the tangent is equal to e. From Fig. 3, we see, that for $0 \leqslant A < e$, the straight line $y = Ax$ has no points in common with the curve $y = e^x$; that is, Eq. (70) cannot have real roots. For $A < 0$, the equation has one real root. Finally, for $A \geqslant e$, it has two and only two real roots. For $A = e$ (the case of the tangent), these roots combine in a single multiple root.* Thus, we have the situation with regard to real roots of Eq. (70) for real values of A.

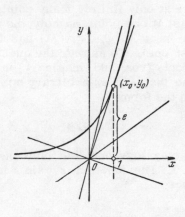

FIG. 3

To show the existence of imaginary roots, we shall not require that A be a real number. For $A = 0$, Eq. (70) has no roots at all, as we know. On the basis of the theorem of this section, there can be no other exceptional value. Therefore, for any $A \neq 0$, Eq. (70) has infinitely many complex roots.

In particular, if A is a real nonzero number, there can be no more than two real roots, as we have just shown. Therefore, Eq. (70) in this case has infinitely many imaginary roots.

The problem as to the number of roots of the equation

$$\sin z = Az \tag{71}$$

is solved in a somewhat more complicated manner because, whereas in the case of Eq. (70) the exceptional value $A = 0$ hits one in the eye, in the present case it is not immediately obvious whether an exceptional value exists or not.

Let us first assume that A is a real number. For $A = 0$, the equation takes the form

---

*That there can be no more than two real roots follows from the fact that the curve $y = e^x$ is a convex (downward) curve and hence cannot be intersected at more than two points by a straight line. On the other hand, the line $y = Ax$, which meets the curve at the first point cannot at the same time remain above the curve (since e^x increases faster than does Ax). Therefore, there must be a second point of intersection.

This equation has infinitely many real roots $z = n\pi$ (where $n = 0$, $\pm 1, \pm 2, \ldots$) and (as we can verify by expressing $\sin z$ in exponential form according to Euler's formula (16)) no imaginary roots at all. If $A \neq 0$, the straight line $y = Ax$ intersects the sinusoid $y = \sin x$ at only finitely many points though it always intersects it at least at one point, namely, the coordinate origin.

Therefore, for real $A \neq 0$, Eq. (71) has finitely many real roots (and at least one). To answer the question regarding the total number of roots (real and imaginary) in the general case, let us now assume that A is an arbitrary complex number. We rewrite Eq. (71) in the form

$$\frac{\sin z}{z} = A. \tag{71$'$}$$

In doing so, we may lose one (but only one) root of Eq. (71), namely, the root 0. The function $z^{-1} \sin z$ is a transcendental entire function since

$$\frac{\sin z}{z} = 1 - \frac{z^2}{3!} + \frac{z^4}{5!} - \frac{z^6}{7!} + \cdots$$

and this series converges everywhere. One can show without difficulty that its order is equal to 1. If we make the substitution $z = \sqrt{\zeta}$, we obtain the entire function

$$\frac{\sin \sqrt{\zeta}}{\sqrt{\zeta}} = 1 - \frac{\zeta}{3!} + \frac{\zeta^2}{5!} - \frac{\zeta^3}{7!} + \frac{\zeta^4}{9!} - \cdots,$$

the order of which is a fraction, namely, $1/2$. Consequently, we can apply the strengthened form of Picard's theorem, given in the preceding section, to the equation

$$\frac{\sin \sqrt{\zeta}}{\sqrt{\zeta}} = A. \tag{71$''$}$$

From this it follows that Eq. (71$''$) has infinitely many roots for arbitrary A. Therefore, (71$'$) also has infinitely many roots $z = \sqrt{\zeta_0}$. From this, we conclude finally that Eq. (71) has infinitely many roots for arbitrary A; that is, there are no exceptional values. For $A \neq 0$, all the roots except finitely many are imaginary.

26. In the preceding section, we considered an equation of the form $f(z) = AP(z)$, where $f(z)$ is a transcendental entire function, $P(z)$ is a polynomial, and A is a complex constant.

Let us, finally, consider the equation

$$f(z) = Ag(z), \tag{72}$$

where $f(z)$ and $g(z)$ are distinct transcendental entire functions. For example, let us consider the equation $\tan z = A$, which can be written in the form $\sin z = A \cos z$, or the equation $e^z = A \sin z$, etc. For such equations we have the following

Theorem. If $f(z)$ and $g(z)$ are two transcendental entire functions the ratio of which is not a rational function (that is, if $f(z)/g(z) \neq P(z)/Q(z)$, where $P(z)$ and $Q(z)$ are polynomials), then Eq. (72) has infinitely many roots for every complex number A with the possible exception of two values for which there may be only finitely many roots or even none at all.

This result can be worded more briefly in terms of the important concept of a meromorphic function. A function $\varphi(z)$ is said to be *meromorphic* if it can be represented as the ratio of two entire functions:

$$\varphi(z) = \frac{f(z)}{g(z)}.$$

The name "meromorphic" comes from the Greek words μέρος (fraction) and μορφή (form).

To this class belong, in particular, rational functions, that is, functions that can be represented as the ratio of two polynomials. It can be shown that no meromorphic function other than a rational function can be algebraic; that is, all other meromorphic functions are transcendental. Examples of transcendental meromorphic functions are:

$$\tan z = \frac{\sin z}{\cos z}; \quad \cot z = \frac{\cos z}{\sin z};$$

$$\sec z = \frac{1}{\cos z}; \quad \csc z = \frac{1}{\sin z}; \quad \frac{1}{e^z - 1}, \text{ etc.}$$

It follows from the definition of a meromorphic function that, in particular, every entire function $f(z)$ is also a meromorphic function since it can be represented in the form of the ratio

$$f(z) = \frac{f(z)}{1}.$$

Obviously, the fundamental theorem of this section applies to roots of an equation of the form

$$\varphi(z) = \frac{f(z)}{g(z)} = A,$$

where $\varphi(z)$ is a meromorphic but not a rational function.

Therefore, this theorem can be formulated as follows:

If $\varphi(z)$ is a transcendental meromorphic function, the equation

$$\varphi(z) = A$$

has infinitely many roots for every complex number A with two possible exceptions.

Let us use the simple example

$$\tan z = A,$$

to show that such an equation can have two exceptional values. By definition, tan z is equal to $(\sin z)/(\cos z)$. If we write the above equation in the form $\sin z = A \cos z$, and write sin z and cos z in their exponential forms (see Eqs. 16)), we obtain

$$\frac{e^{iz} - e^{-iz}}{2i} = A \frac{e^{iz} + e^{-iz}}{2},$$

from which we get

$$(1 - Ai) e^{iz} = (1 + Ai) e^{-iz}.$$

If we multiply both sides by e^{iz} (which is a nonzero complex number), we reduce Eq. (73) to the form

$$(1 - Ai) e^{2iz} = 1 + Ai. \tag{73'}$$

If $A = i$, the equation takes the form

$$2e^{2iz} = 0, \quad \text{or} \quad e^{2iz} = 0.$$

We know that this equation has no roots. Therefore, Eq. (73) also has no roots when $A = i$.

If $A = -i$, Eq. (73') takes the form

$$0 \cdot e^{2iz} = 2,$$

which obviously has no roots. Therefore, Eq. (73) has no roots when $A = -i$.

Thus, we have found two exceptional values $+i$ and $-i$ for Eq. (73). On the basis of the theorem in this section, no other value of A can be exceptional. To see this directly, suppose that $A \neq \pm i$. Then, Eq. (73') can be represented in the form

$$e^{2iz} = B, \tag{73''}$$

where $B = (1 + Ai)/(1 - Ai) \neq 0$. If we take the logarithms of both sides (see Section 8), we obtain

$$2iz = \operatorname{Ln} B,$$

from which we get

$$z = \frac{1}{2i} \operatorname{Ln} B,$$

or

$$z = \frac{1}{2i} \operatorname{Ln} \frac{1 + Ai}{1 - Ai}. \tag{74}$$

Since the logarithm on the right has infinitely many values, this equation shows that Eq. (73) has infinitely many roots.

Suppose, for example, that $A = 1$, so that we are speaking of the solution of the simple equation

$$\tan z = 1.$$

From formula (74), we obtain

$$z = \frac{1}{2i} \operatorname{Ln} \frac{1+i}{1-i} = \frac{1}{2i} \operatorname{Ln} \frac{(1+i)^2}{(1-i)(1+i)} =$$
$$= \frac{1}{2i} \operatorname{Ln} \frac{2i}{2} = \frac{1}{2i} \operatorname{Ln} i.$$

But, from formula (22′), we have

$$\operatorname{Ln} i = \ln |i| + i (\arg i + 2n\pi) =$$
$$= \ln 1 + i \left(\frac{\pi}{2} + 2n\pi \right) = i \left(\frac{\pi}{2} + 2n\pi \right),$$
$$n = 0, \pm 1, \pm 2, \ldots.$$

Finally, we have

$$z = \frac{1}{2i} i \left(\frac{\pi}{2} + 2n\pi \right) = \frac{\pi}{4} + n\pi, \qquad n = 0, \pm 1, \pm 2, \ldots.$$

All these roots of the equation $\tan z = 1$ are known from our elementary courses in mathematics. However, these calculations provide us with one other bit of information, namely, the fact that the equation $\tan z = 1$ has no imaginary roots.

27. We shall not go into an account of the methods of actually finding roots of equations. These equations are taken up in texts on approximation calculations.* We confine ourselves to an example of calculating the asymptotic values of the roots of the equation

$$e^z = Az \quad (A \neq 0),\tag{70}$$

that is, to a derivation of simple approximate formulas for roots.

We noted in Section 25 that Eq. (70) has an infinite set of roots for arbitrary nonzero A. We note also that, for every A, all these roots can be arranged in a sequence that approaches ∞ (see Section 21). For simplicity, let us assume that A is a real positive number. Then, it follows from (70) that, for an arbitrary root $z = x + iy$ of this equation, we have

$$|e^z| = A\,|z|,$$

or

$$e^x = A\sqrt{x^2 + y^2}.\tag{70'}$$

But the absolute values of the roots approach infinity:

$$(|z| = \sqrt{x^2 + y^2} \to +\infty).$$

Therefore, e^x also approaches $+\infty$ and hence $x \to +\infty$. If we rewrite (70') in the form

$$\left(\frac{y}{e^x}\right)^2 = \frac{1}{A^2} - \left(\frac{x}{e^x}\right)^2\tag{70''}$$

and note that $x/e^x \to 0$ as $x \to +\infty$, we conclude that $|y|/e^x \to 1/A$, that is, that the following asymptotic equation** is valid for the real and imaginary parts of the roots of Eq. (70):

$$|y| \approx \frac{1}{A}\,e^x.$$

If we substitute the value of the root $z = x + iy$ into (70), we obtain

---

*See, for example, V. P. Demidovich and I. A. Maron, *Osnovy vychislitel'noy matematiki* (Fundamentals of Computational Mathematics), Moscow, Fizmatgiz, 1963, Chapter IV.

**Variables are said to be asymptotically equal if the limit of their ratio is 1.

$$e^{x+iy} = A(x+iy),$$

or

$$e^x e^{iy} = e^x(\cos y + i \sin y) = A(x+iy).$$

If we now equate the real and imaginary parts, we obtain

$$e^x \cos y = Ax, \quad e^x \sin y = Ay. \qquad (70''')$$

We now replace Eq. (70) by the system (70'''), which is equivalent to it. It was shown above the the real parts of the roots approach $+\infty$. Therefore, for roots of the equation of sufficiently high absolute value, we may assume that $x > 0$. From Eqs. (70'''), it is obvious that, for any pair of numbers (x, y) that satisfies these equations, the pair $(x, -y)$ also satisfies it. This means that the complex roots of Eq. (70) are located symmetrically about the real axis; that is, they come in complex conjugate pairs. Therefore, we can speak of a sequence of roots for which $y > 0$ and another sequence (symmetric to it) for which $y < 0$.

Let us begin by examining the roots for which $y > 0$. For these roots, we have, on the basis of the asymptotic equation proven above,

$$y \approx \frac{1}{A} e^x.$$

Therefore, the second of Eqs. (70''') yields

$$\sin y \approx 1,$$

and this means that

$$y = \frac{\pi}{2} + 2n\pi - \varepsilon_n,$$

where $\varepsilon_n \to 0$ as $n \to \infty$ (with n assuming positive integral values). If we substitute this value of y into the first of Eqs. (70'''), we obtain

$$e^x \sin \varepsilon_n = Ax \quad \text{or} \quad \sin \varepsilon_n = \frac{Ax}{e^x}.$$

Since $\sin \varepsilon_n \approx \varepsilon_n$, we have the asymptotic equation

$$\varepsilon_n \approx \frac{Ax}{e^x} \approx \frac{Ax}{Ay} = \frac{x}{y} \approx \frac{\ln(Ay)}{y}.$$

But it follows from the formula that we found above for y that $y \approx 2n\pi$ and, consequently,

$$\varepsilon_n \approx \frac{\ln (2A\pi n)}{2\pi n}.$$

Thus,*

$$y \approx \frac{\pi}{2} + 2\pi n - \frac{\ln (2A\pi n)}{2\pi n},$$

$$x \approx \ln (Ay) = \ln \left[2A\pi n + \frac{A\pi}{2} - A \frac{\ln (2A\pi n)}{2\pi n} \right] =$$

$$= \ln (2A\pi n) + \ln \left[1 + \frac{1}{4n} - \frac{\ln (2A\pi n)}{4\pi^2 n^2} \right] \approx$$

$$\approx \ln (2A\pi n) + \frac{1}{4n}.$$

Therefore, we obtain for the roots of Eq. (70) the asymptotic formula

$$z = x + iy \approx \ln (2A\pi n) + \frac{1}{4n} \pm i \left[2\pi n + \frac{\pi}{2} - \frac{\ln (2A\pi n)}{2\pi n} \right],$$

where n assumes positive integral values. (We have represented in a single formula both sequences of roots with positive and negative imaginary parts.) The reader can convince himself by means of a substitution that Eq. (70) is approximately satisfied for the values of z that we have found (with an accuracy up to quantities of the order of $n^{-1} \ln n$, which becomes infinitesimal as $n \to \infty$).

The formulas that we have found can also be used for the equation

$$\sin z = Az \quad \text{(for } A > 0\text{)}. \tag{71}$$

Here, the roots $z = x + iy$ come in pairs symmetric about the coordinate origin and $|y|$ increases without bound as we take values of z farther and farther from the coordinate origin. From this it follows that we need only consider the sequence of roots for which $y < 0$ (at a sufficiently great distance from the coordinate origin). The other sequence is obtained by simultaneously

---

*We apply the known formula

$$\ln (1 + \varepsilon) \approx \varepsilon \quad \textbf{as} \quad \varepsilon \to 0,$$

with $\epsilon = \frac{1}{4n} - \frac{\ln (2A\pi n)}{4\pi^2 n^2}$ then and discard the term $- \frac{\ln (2A\pi n)}{4\pi^2 n^2}$, which is infinitesi-mally small in comparison with $1/4n$.

changing the signs of x and y. If we write sin z in its exponential form, we can put Eq. (70) in the form

$$e^{iz} - e^{-iz} = 2Aiz,$$

or, replacing iz with the new unknown w,

$$e^w - e^{-w} = 2Aw. \qquad (71')$$

Here, $w = iz = -y + ix$ and $|e^{-w}| = |e^{y-ix}| = e^y \to 0$ as $y \to -\infty$. If we discard the infinitesimal quantity e^{-w}, we obtain the following simplified equation for obtaining an approximate value of the roots:

$$e^w = 2Aw.$$

When we compare this equation with Eq. (70), we see that w can be represented by an asymptotic formula of the form

$$w = u + iv \approx \ln(4A\pi n) + \frac{1}{4n} \pm i\left[2\pi n + \frac{\pi}{2} - \frac{\ln(4A\pi n)}{2\pi n}\right].$$

Therefore, for $z = w/i = -iw$, we obtain

$$z \approx \pm\left[2\pi n + \frac{\pi}{2} - \frac{\ln(4A\pi n)}{2\pi n}\right] - i\left[\ln(4A\pi n) + \frac{1}{4n}\right],$$

where n assumes positive integral values. Since the roots are symmetrically distributed about the coordinate origin, we need to put the symbol $\pm$ (independent of the one preceding the real part) in front of the imaginary part.

CHAPTER 5 ————————————————

Algebraic Relationships and
Addition Theorems

28. We have seen that a nonpolynomial entire function $f(z)$ cannot satisfy any algebraic equation (cf. Section 16). For just that reason, such functions are called transcendental. However, two transcendental entire functions can be related by an algebraic equation. A very simple example of this is that of the functions sin z and cos z, which satisfy the relation

$$\sin^2 z + \cos^2 z = 1. \tag{75}$$

Let us consider the more general relation

$$[f(z)]^n + [g(z)]^n = 1, \tag{76}$$

where n is an integer ≥ 2, and let us see if we can find all entire functions that satisfy it.

We begin with the case $n = 2$. Might there be other entire functions that sin z and cos z that are related by this equation? Since (75) is an identity in z, it remains valid if we replace z by any entire function. Thus, for example, we may write

$$\sin^2 (1 - z + 2z^3) + \cos^2 (1 - z + 2z^3) = 1,$$

$$\sin^2 (e^z) + \cos^2 (e^z) = 1.$$

And, in general, for any entire function $h(z)$,

$$\sin^2 [h(z)] + \cos^2 [h(z)] = 1.$$

Since an entire function of an entire function is an entire function (see Section 5), we obtain the following result:

There exist infinitely many pairs of entire functions

$$\sin[h(z)] \quad \text{and} \quad \cos[h(z)] \tag{77}$$

(where $h(z)$ is any entire function) that are related by the algebraic relationship (75).

Let us now prove the validity of the converse to this:

If $f(z)$ and $g(z)$ are two entire functions satisfying the equation

$$[f(z)]^2 + [g(z)]^2 = 1, \tag{78}$$

then there exists an entire function $h(z)$ such that $f(z) = \cos[h(z)]$ and $g(z) = \sin[h(z)]$.

Proof: Let us rewrite Eq. (78) in the form

$$[f(z) + ig(z)][f(z) - ig(z)] = 1. \tag{78'}$$

From this it is clear that $f(z) + ig(z)$ is an entire function that does not vanish for any z. Therefore (see Section 9), there exists an entire function (and we represent it by $ih(z)$ such that

$$f(z) + ig(z) = e^{ih(z)}, \tag{79}$$

and hence

$$f(z) - ig(z) = \frac{1}{f(z) + ig(z)} = e^{-ih(z)}. \tag{80}$$

It follows from (79) and (80) that

$$f(z) = \frac{e^{ih(z)} + e^{-ih(z)}}{2} = \cos[h(z)],$$

$$g(z) = \frac{e^{ih(z)} - e^{-ih(z)}}{2i} = \sin[h(z)],$$

which completes the proof.

29. Let us return to the general equation

$$[f(z)]^n + [g(z)]^n = 1, \tag{76}$$

where $n \geqslant 3$, and let us prove the theorem discovered by the French mathematician Montel that

Equation (76) is satisfied by no pair of nonconstant entire functions.

As a preliminary, let us find the decomposition of a binomial of the form $x^n + 1$ into linear factors. To do this, we need only find all n roots of the equation $x^n + 1 = 0$, that is, of the equation $x^n = -1$. These roots are

$$x_k = \cos \frac{\pi + 2k\pi}{n} + i \sin \frac{\pi + 2k\pi}{n}, \quad k = 0, 1, 2, \ldots, n-1.$$

This expression does provide all the roots since the values of x_k are all distinct, there are n of them, and each satisfies the condition $x_k^n = -1$.

If for brevity, we set $x_0 = \cos(\pi/n) + i \sin(\pi/n) = \varepsilon$, we have

$$x_k = \left(\cos \frac{\pi}{n} + i \sin \frac{\pi}{n} \right)^{2k+1} = \varepsilon^{2k+1}, \quad k = 0, 1, \ldots, n-1.$$

Therefore,

$$x^n + 1 = (x - x_0) \ldots (x - x_{n-1}) =$$
$$= (x - \varepsilon)(x - \varepsilon^3) \ldots (x - \varepsilon^{2n-1}).$$

If we now replace x by the quotient $f(z)/g(z)$ and multiply both sides by $[g(z)]^n$, we obtain the identity

$$[f(z)]^n + [g(z)]^n =$$
$$= [f(z) - \varepsilon g(z)][f(z) - \varepsilon^3 g(z)][f(z) - \varepsilon^5 g(z)] \ldots \quad (81)$$
$$\ldots [f(z) - \varepsilon^{2n-1} g(z)].$$

It follows from Eq. (76) that none of the factors in the right-hand member of (81) can vanish for any z. Since each of them is an entire function, we conclude (cf. Section 9) that there exist entire functions $h_0(z)$ $h_1(z), \ldots, h_{n-1}(z)$ such that

$$f(z) - \varepsilon g(z) = e^{h_0(z)}, \qquad f(z) - \varepsilon^3 g(z) = e^{h_1(z)},$$
$$f(z) - \varepsilon^5 g(z) = e^{h_2(z)}, \ldots, f(z) - \varepsilon^{2n-1} g(z) = e^{h_{n-1}(z)}. \quad (82)$$

Let us consider the first three of these equations (there are, in all, n such equations, and we are assuming that $n \geqslant 3$). If we subtract the second from the first and the third from the second, we obtain

$$(\varepsilon^3 - \varepsilon) g(z) = e^{h_0(z)} - e^{h_1(z)},$$
$$(\varepsilon^5 - \varepsilon^3) g(z) = e^{h_1(z)} - e^{h_2(z)}. \quad (83)$$

We note that

$$\varepsilon = \cos \frac{\pi}{n} + i \sin \frac{\pi}{n} \neq 0 \quad \text{and} \quad \varepsilon^2 = \cos \frac{2\pi}{n} + i \sin \frac{2\pi}{n} \neq \pm 1$$

(since $n \geqslant 3$). Therefore, it follows from the identities (83) that

$$\frac{e^{h_0(z)} - e^{h_1(z)}}{\varepsilon\,(\varepsilon^2 - 1)} = \frac{e^{h_1(z)} - e^{h_2(z)}}{\varepsilon^3\,(\varepsilon^2 - 1)},$$

or

$$\varepsilon^2 e^{h_0(z)} + e^{h_2(z)} = (1 + \varepsilon^2)\,e^{h_1(z)}.$$

Let us write this equation in the form

$$\left[\frac{\varepsilon}{\sqrt{1 + \varepsilon^2}}\, e^{-\frac{h_0'(z) - h_1(z)}{2}}\right]^2 + \left[\frac{1}{\sqrt{1 + \varepsilon^2}} \cdot e^{\frac{h_2(z) - h_1(z)}{2}}\right]^2 = 1.$$

Since the functions in the square brackets are entire functions, it follows from the theorem of Section 28 that there must exist an entire function $h(z)$ such that

and

$$\left.\begin{array}{l}\dfrac{\varepsilon}{\sqrt{1 + \varepsilon^2}}\, e^{\frac{h_0(z) - h_1(z)}{2}} = \cos[h(z)] \\[4mm] \dfrac{1}{\sqrt{1 + \varepsilon^2}}\, e^{\frac{h_2(z) - h_1(z)}{2}} = \sin[h(z)].\end{array}\right\} \tag{84}$$

Let us show that $h(z)$ is a constant. If we assume the opposite, then $h(z)$ must be either a polynomial of degree no less than 1 or a transcendental entire function. In the first case, there exists a value $z = z_0$ such that $h(z) = \pi/2$ (on the basis of the fundamental theorem of algebra). For $z = z_0$, the left side of the first of Eqs. (84) is nonzero and the right side is equal to zero, which is impossible. In the second case, according to Picard's little theorem (see Section 24), at least one of the two equations $h(z) = \pi/2$, $h(z) = -\pi/2$ must have roots (in fact, infinitely many roots). If z_0 is one of these roots, substitution of z_0 into the first of Eqs. (84) again produces a contradiction.

Thus, we have shown that $h(z)$ is a constant. It follows from Eqs. (84) that the exponents in the expressions on the left sides are also constants:

$$\frac{h_0(z) - h_1(z)}{2} \equiv a, \qquad \frac{h_2(z) - h_1(z)}{2} \equiv b.$$

But the first of Eqs. (83) yields

$$g(z) = \frac{e^{h_0(z)} - e^{h_1(z)}}{\varepsilon\,(\varepsilon^2 - 1)} = e^{h_1(z)}\,\frac{e^{h_0(z) - h_1(z)} - 1}{\varepsilon\,(\varepsilon^2 - 1)} =$$
$$= e^{h_1(z)}\,\frac{e^{2a} - 1}{\varepsilon\,(\varepsilon^2 - 1)} = \alpha e^{h_1(z)}, \tag{85}$$

where $\alpha = (e^{2a} - 1)/\varepsilon\,(\varepsilon^2 - 1)$ is a constant. On the other hand, it follows from the second of Eqs. (82) that

$$f(z) = \varepsilon^3 g(z) + e^{h_1(z)} = (\varepsilon^3\alpha + 1)\, e^{h_1(z)} = \beta e^{h_1(z)}, \tag{86}$$

where $\beta = \varepsilon^3\alpha + 1$.

Substituting these expressions for $f(z)$ and $g(z)$ into Eq. (76), we obtain

$$(\alpha^n + \beta^n)\, e^{h_1(z)} = 1,$$

that is,

$$e^{h_1(z)} = \frac{1}{\alpha^n + \beta^n} = \gamma$$

is a constant. When we compare (85) and (86), we see that $f(z)$ and $g(z)$ are also constants. This completes the proof of Montel's theorem.

Summarizing the results of the last two sections, we have the following:

If two entire functions $f(z)$ and $g(z)$ satisfy an algebraic relation of the form

$$[f(z)]^n + [g(z)]^n = 1,$$

where n is an integer $\geqslant 2$, then, for $n = 2$, these functions are necessarily of the form

$$f(z) = \cos\,[h(z)], \quad g(z) = \sin\,[h(z)],$$

where $h(z)$ is an entire function, and, for $n \geqslant 3$, they are both constants.

We note that the proof given above for Montel's theorem can be applied almost without change to proving the following more general

Theorem. There do not exist two entire functions $f(z)$ and $g(z)$, at least one nonconstant, that satisfy an equation of the form

$$a_0\,[f(z)]^n + a_1\,[f(z)]^{n-1}\,g(z) + \dots + a_n\,[g(z)]^n = b,$$

where $n \geqslant 3$, $b \neq 0$, and the equation $a_0 x^n + a_1 x^{n-1} + \dots + a_n = 0$ has at least three distinct nonzero roots.

Proof: Let us denote by $x_0, x_1, \dots, x_{n-1}$ the roots of the last equation. Then, we can rewrite the given relationship between the entire functions in the form

$$\frac{a_0}{b}\,[f\,(z) - x_0 g\,(z)]\,[f\,(z) - x_1 g\,(z)]\,[f\,(z) - x_2 g\,(z)] \cdots$$
$$\cdots\,[f\,(z) - x_{n-1} g\,(z)] = 1$$

and apply to the three distinct factors

$$f\,(z) - x_0 g\,(z), \quad f\,(z) - x_1 g\,(z), \quad f\,(z) - x_2 g\,(z)$$

the above reasoning, which shows that $f(z)$ and $g(z)$ are both constants.

30. We shall not go into the various other algebraic relationships between *distinct* entire functions. Let us turn to algebraic relationships between values of a *single* entire function *at different values* of its argument.

Let us begin with the simplest of these, namely, the equation for the periodicity of an entire function

$$f\,(z + \omega) = f\,(z),$$

where ω is a constant, known as the *period* of the function $f(z)$. Examples of periodic entire functions are the exponential function e^z (with period $2\pi i$), the trigonometric functions $\cos z$ and $\sin z$ (with period 2π), etc. If ω is any complex number other than zero, the simplest example of an entire function with period ω is the exponential function $Ce^{2\pi i z/\omega}$, where $C \neq 0$. Obviously, a constant can be regarded as a periodic function the period of which is any complex number. Let us show that no nonconstant polynomial can be a periodic function. As we know, $P(z) \to \infty$ as $z \to \infty$. Suppose that $\omega \neq 0$ is the period of the polynomial. If z_0 is any complex number, then

$$P\,(z_0) = P\,(z_0 + \omega) = P\,(z_0 + 2\omega) = \ldots = P\,(z_0 + n\omega) = \ldots.$$

Obviously, $z_0 + n\omega \to \infty$ as $n \to \infty$. Consequently, $P(z_0 + n\omega) \to \infty$ as $n \to \infty$. But this conclusion is incompatible with the fact that the value $P(z_0 + n\omega)$ is constant, specifically, equal to $P(z_0)$. Thus, *a nonconstant entire function $f(z)$ can be periodic only if it is transcendental.*

With the aid of exponential functions, we can construct infinitely many entire functions. For example, let $n_1, n_2, \ldots, n_k$ denote distinct integers. Then, each of the entire functions

$$e^{\frac{2\pi i}{\omega} n_1 z}, \quad e^{\frac{2\pi i}{\omega} n_2 z}, \quad \ldots, \quad e^{\frac{2\pi i}{\omega} n_k z}$$

is periodic with period ω. If we multiply these by arbitrary complex numbers $A_1, A_2, \ldots, A_k$ (some of which may be zero) and add, we obtain a new entire function with period ω:

$$f(z) = \sum_{j=1}^{k} A_j e^{\frac{2\pi i}{\omega} n_j z}.$$

Functions of this sort are called trigonometric *polynomials*. This name is easily justified. If we replace the exponential functions with trigonometric functions according to the formula

$$e^{\frac{2\pi i}{\omega} n_j z} = \cos\left(\frac{2\pi}{\omega} n_j z\right) + i \sin\left(\frac{2\pi}{\omega} n_j z\right),$$

we represent $f(z)$ in the form

$$f(z) = \sum_{j=1}^{k} \left[A_j \cos\left(\frac{2\pi}{\omega} n_j z\right) + i A_j \sin\left(\frac{2\pi}{\omega} n_j z\right) \right].$$

Let us suppose, in particular, that $n_1 = -p$, $n_2 = -p+1$, ... , $n_k = p$, where p is any nonnegative integer. (The numbers n_1, n_2, ... , n_k range from $-p$ to p each greater by 1 than the preceding; obviously, $k = 2p + 1$). Then, the trigonometric polynomial takes the form

$$f(z) = \sum_{-p}^{+p} A_j e^{\frac{2\pi i}{\omega} n_j z},$$

or

$$f(z) = \sum_{-p}^{p} \left[A_j \cos\left(\frac{2\pi}{\omega} jz\right) + i A_j \sin\left(\frac{2\pi}{\omega} jz\right) \right].$$

Taking advantage of the facts that the cosine is an even function and the sine is an odd function, we can also write this last sum in the form

$$f(z) = A_0 + \sum_{j=1}^{p} \left[(A_j + A_{-j}) \cos\left(\frac{2\pi}{\omega} jz\right) + \right.$$
$$\left. + (iA_j - iA_{-j}) \sin\left(\frac{2\pi}{\omega} jz\right) \right].$$

Setting $A_j + A_{-j} = a_j$ and $iA_j - iA_{-j} = b_j$, we finally write the trigonometric polynomial in the form

$$f(z) = A_0 + \sum_{j=1}^{p} \left[a_j \cos\left(\frac{2\pi}{\omega} jz\right) + b_j \sin\left(\frac{2\pi}{\omega} jz\right) \right].$$

Here, if at least one of the numbers a_p and b_p is nonzero (and this means that at least one of the numbers A_p and A_{-p} is nonzero), then p is called the *order* of the trigonometric polynomial. If $p = 0$, we obtain a constant as a special case of a trigonometric polynomial.

The following theorem characterizes trigonometric polynomials in the class of all periodic entire functions:

Theorem. If a periodic entire function $f(z)$ with nonzero period w satisfies an inequality of the form

$$|f(z)| \leqslant C e^{\gamma \frac{2\pi}{|\omega|}|z|}$$

for some $C > 0$ and $\gamma \geqslant 0$ and for all sufficiently large $|z|$ (where $|z| > R_0$), then $f(z)$ is a trigonometric polynomial of order not exceeding $p = [\gamma]$ (where $[\gamma]$ denotes the greatest integer not exceeding γ).

In particular, if $0 \leqslant \gamma < 1$, then $p = [\gamma] = 0$, Therefore, for $\gamma < 1$, the function $f(z)$ is a constant.

If a periodic entire function with period ω is not a trigonometric polynomial, it can be expressed in the form of the sum of an everywhere-convergent series of the form

$$f(z) = \sum_{-\infty}^{+\infty} A_n e^{\frac{2\pi i}{\omega} nz},$$

which can also be represented in the form of a trigonometric series

$$f(z) = a_0 + \left[a_1 \cos \left(\frac{2\pi}{\omega} z \right) + b_1 \sin \left(\frac{2\pi}{\omega} z \right) \right] + \ldots$$
$$\ldots + \left[a_n \cos \left(\frac{2\pi}{\omega} z \right) + b_n \sin \left(\frac{2\pi}{\omega} z \right) \right] + \ldots . \tag{87}$$

Infinitely many of the coefficients in the expression for $f(z)$ are nonzero.

The converse theorem is also true. Every everywhere-convergent series of this form represents a periodic entire function with period ω. Here, this periodic entire function will not be a trigonometric polynomial if infinitely many of its coefficients are nonzero.

Proofs of these assertions appear in Section 2 of the Appendix.

31. Of course, every function with period ω also has other periods: $-\omega, 2\omega, -2\omega, \ldots$. In general, any integral multiple of ω is a period of $f(z)$. Thus, for example,

$$f(z-3\omega)=f[(z-3\omega)+\omega]=f(z-2\omega)=$$
$$=f[(z-2\omega)+\omega]=f(z-\omega)=f[(z-\omega)+\omega]=f(z),$$

from which it follows that -3ω is also a period of $f(z)$.

Let $k\omega$ and $l\omega$ denote any two periods of $f(z)$. Then, their ratio is the rational number l/k.

However, we may ask whether it is possible for an entire function $f(z)$ to have two periods ω_1 and ω_2 the ratio of which is not a rational number. It turns out that the answer to this question is negative unless $f(z)$ is a constant. In other words, *no nonconstant entire function has two periods the ratio of which is not a rational number.*

We divide the proof of this proposition into two cases.

Let us assume first that the ratio $\omega_2/\omega_1=\alpha$ is a real irrational number. Let n denote an arbitrary natural number and p_n denote the greatest integer not exceeding $n\alpha$. Then, $0 < n\alpha - p_n < 1$, from which we get $|n\omega_2 - p_n\omega_1| = |n\alpha - p_n||\omega_1| < |\omega_1|$.

Obviously, if $m \neq n$, then $m\omega_2 - p_m\omega_1 \neq n\omega_2 - p_n\omega_1$ (because if we assume that $m\omega_2 - p_m\omega_1 = n\omega_2 - p_n\omega_1$, we obtain $\alpha = \omega_2/\omega_1 = p_m - p_n/m - n$, which is irrational in contradiction with our hypothesis). Therefore, all points of the infinite set

$$\omega_2 - p_1\omega_1,\ 2\omega_2 - p_2\omega_1,\ \ldots,\ n\omega_2 - p_n\omega_1,\ldots$$

are distinct and they lie in the disk of radius $|\omega_1|$ with center at the origin. But the periodic function $f(z)$ assumes the same value $f(n\omega_2 - p_n\omega_1) = f(0)$ at all of them (since ω_2 and ω_1 are periods of $f(z)$). On the basis of what was said in Section 21, it follows from this that $f(z) \equiv f(0)$, which means that $f(z)$ is a constant.

Now, let us consider the case in which ω_2/ω_1 is not a real number. It follows from this assumption that the vectors representing ω_1 and ω_2 drawn through a single point z_0 (any value will do for this) define a parallelogram P (see Fig. 4). It follows from the periodicity of the function $f(z)$ that the value assumed by it at an arbitrary point in the z-plane is also assumed at any point z' in this parallelogram that is related to z by an equation of the form

$$z = z' + m_1\omega_1 + m_2\omega_2$$

where m_1 and m_2 are integers. Specifically,

$$f(z) = f(z' + m_1\omega_1 + m_2\omega_2) = f(z'),$$

since ω_1 and ω_2 are periods of $f(z)$. Therefore, if all the values of $|f(z)|$ in the parallelogram P are less than or equal to some positive number M (such a number exists since the function $f(z)$ is continuous and hence bounded in P), then, at an arbitrary point in the plane,

$$|f(z)| \leqslant M.$$

In other words, the entire function $f(z)$ is bounded in the complex plane. But we know from Liouville's theorem (see Section 14) that such a function must be a constant. This completes the proof of our proposition.

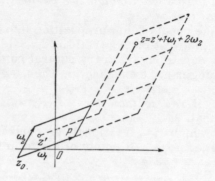

FIG. 4

Instead of the class of entire functions, we may consider the broader class of meromorphic functions (see Section 26). It turns out that there are nonconstant meromorphic periodic functions possessing periods ω_1 and ω_2 the ratio of which is an *imaginary* number. Such functions are called *doubly-periodic* or *elliptic* functions. The values that they assume in the period parallelogram defined by the vectors ω_1 and ω_2 are repeated throughout the entire complex plane.

32. As a generalization of the relation

$$f(z + \omega) = f(z)$$

we can consider a relation of the form

$$f(z + \omega) = af(z) \qquad (\omega \neq 0, \ a \neq 0). \tag{88}$$

It is easy to exhibit an entire function satisfying this relationship. Such a function is the exponential function $\varphi(z) = e^{\frac{\ln a}{\omega} z}$, where $\ln a$ is the principal value of the logarithm of a (cf. Section 8, formula $(22'')$). Obviously,

$$e^{\frac{\ln a}{\omega}(z+\omega)} = e^{\frac{\ln a}{\omega}z+\ln a} = e^{\ln a}\, e^{\frac{\ln a}{\omega}z} = ae^{\frac{\ln a}{\omega}z},$$

that is, the function $\varphi(z)$ does indeed satisfy Eq. (88):

$$\varphi(z+\omega) = a\varphi(z). \tag{88$'$}$$

If we divide (88) by (88$'$), we obtain

$$f(z+\omega) : \varphi(z+\omega) = f(z) : \varphi(z).$$

From this it follows that the ratio $f(z)/\varphi(z)$ is a function $g(z)$ with period ω. Here, $g(z)$ is an entire function since $\varphi(z)$ does not vanish anywhere. Thus,

$$f(z) = \varphi(z)\, g(z) = e^{\frac{\ln a}{\omega}z}\, g(z),$$

that is, every entire function that satisfies (88) is the product of the exponential function $e\,(\ln a)z/\omega$ and some period function $g(z)$ with period ω.

We introduce the notations

$$f(z) = u,\ f(z+\omega) = v.$$

Then, Eq. (88) takes the form

$$u - av = 0. \tag{88$''$}$$

This is a linear relationship between u and v. At first glance, one might think that we can obtain a significant generalization of the problem that we have been considering if we seek entire functions satisfying not the linear equation (88$''$) but the algebraic homogeneous equation of arbitrary degree n:

$$a_0 u^n + a_1 u^{n-1}v + a_2 u^{n-2}v^2 + \ldots + a_n v^n = 0,\ n \geqslant 1, \tag{88$'''$}$$

where, for definiteness, we assume $a_0 \neq 0$. However, the polynomial in the left-hand member of the equation can always be decomposed into factors

$$a_0(u - x_0 v)(u - x_1 v)\ldots(u - x_{n-1}v) = 0.$$

Therefore, everything reduces to satisfying one of the conditions of the form

$$u - x_k v = 0 \qquad (u = f(z + \omega), \qquad v = f(z)),$$

and we have already considered this case.

33. An interesting and important type of algebraic relation between *three* values of a function is provided by the so-called algebraic addition theorems.

A function $f(z)$ (it is assumed that this is an analytic function and, in our present exposition, that it is an entire function) is said to possess or to obey an algebraic addition theorem if, for arbitrary z_1 and z_2, the values of the function $f(z_1) = u, f(z_2) = v$, and $f(z_1 + z_2) = w$ are related by an algebraic relation of the form

$$P(u, v, w) = 0 \tag{89}$$

where $(P(u, v, w)$ is a polynomial in the three variables u, v, and w.

The simplest example of an entire function possessing an addition theorem is the linear function

$$f(z) = az.$$

Here, $u = az_1$, $v = az_2$, and $w = a(z_1 + z_2)$. Obviously,

$$w = u + v$$

or

$$w - u - v = 0.$$

Therefore, in the present case, we may set $P(u, v, w) = w - u - v$.
Another example is the function

$$f(z) = az^2.$$

Here, $u = az_1^2, v = az_2^2, w = a(z_1 + z_2)^2$. Therefore, $w = u + v + 2\sqrt{uv}$ or, getting rid of the radical, we have

$$(w - u - v)^2 - 4uv = 0.$$

Here, $P(u, v, w) = (w - u - v)^2 - 4uv$ is a second-degree polynomial in u, v, and w.

A more general case is the function $f(z) = az^n$, where n is an integer $\geqslant 2$. Here, $u = az_1^n$, $v = az_2^n$, and $w = a(z_1 + z_2)^n$, so that $\sqrt[n]{w} = \sqrt[n]{u} + \sqrt[n]{v}$. Again, we might get rid of the radicals and obtain the corresponding polynomial $P(u, v, w)$. However, it is not actually necessary to carry out these calculations. It is more convenient to keep the addition theorem for the present case in the present very simple form (that is, with the radicals).

In the case of the exponential function e^z, the addition theorem takes, as we know (see Section 7), the following form:

$$e^{z_1} e^{z_2} = e^{z_1 + z_2};$$

which in our notations, is $w - uv = 0$. Here, $P(u, v, w) = w - uv$ is a second-degree polynomial.

Let us look again at the functions $\cos z$ and $\sin z$. Since these functions are expressed in terms of exponentials, the addition theorems for them can be derived from the addition theorem for the exponential function.

This is done most simply by using Euler's formula $e^{iz} = \cos z + i \sin z$. Thus, we have

$$e^{i(z_1 + z_2)} = \cos(z_1 + z_2) + i \sin(z_1 + z_2). \tag{90}$$

On the other hand,

$$e^{i(z_1 + z_2)} = e^{iz_1} e^{iz_2} = (\cos z_1 + i \sin z_1)(\cos z_2 + i \sin z_2) =$$
$$= (\cos z_1 \cos z_2 - \sin z_1 \sin z_2) +$$
$$+ i(\sin z_1 \cos z_2 + \sin z_2 \cos z_1). \tag{91}$$

Equating these two expressions, we obtain

$$\cos(z_1 + z_2) + i \sin(z_1 + z_2) = \cos z_1 \cos z_2 - \sin z_1 \sin z_2 +$$
$$+ i(\sin z_1 \cos z_2 + \sin z_2 \cos z_1). \tag{92}$$

Since $\cos(z_1 + z_2)$ and $\sin(z_1 + z_2)$ are not real numbers in the general case, we can not obtain the desired formulas by equating what seem to be the real and imaginary parts in this equation. We achieve our goal by taking advantage of the fact that the cosine is an even and the sine an odd function (cf. Section 7). If we replace z_1 with $-z_1$ and z_2 with $-z_2$ and use these two facts, we obtain

$$\cos(z_1 + z_2) - i \sin(z_1 + z_2) = \cos z_1 \cos z_2 - \sin z_1 \sin z_2 -$$
$$- i(\sin z_1 \cos z_2 + \sin z_2 \cos z_1). \tag{93}$$

Finally, by adding (92) and (93) in the one case and by subtracting (93) from (92) in the second case and (in both cases) dividing by 2, we obtain the formulas

$$\cos(z_1 + z_2) = \cos z_1 \cos z_2 - \sin z_1 \sin z_2, \qquad (94)$$

$$\sin(z_1 + z_2) = \sin z_1 \cos z_2 + \sin z_2 \cos z_1 \qquad (95)$$

(which are well known from elementary trigonometry). For $z_1 = z$ and $z_2 = -z$, the first of these yields

$$1 = \cos^2 z + \sin^2 z. \qquad (96)$$

In external appearance, formulas (94) and (95) are different from the addition theorems that we have been considering up to now. Specifically, the value of $\cos(z_1 + z_2)$, for example, is expressed not only in terms of $\cos z_1$ and $\cos z_2$, as we would wish it to be, but also in terms of the values of another function, namely, the values $\sin z_1$ and $\sin z_2$. Formula (96), however, comes to our aid. If, just as before, we set $\cos z_1 = u$, $\cos z_2 = v$, and $\cos(z_1 + z_2) = w$, we obtain

$$\sin z_1 = \sqrt{1 - u^2}, \quad \sin z_2 = \sqrt{1 - v^2}.$$

Therefore, formula (94) takes the form

$$w = uv - \sqrt{1 - u^2} \ \sqrt{1 - v^2}.$$

We need only get rid of the radicals to represent the addition theorem for $\cos z$ in a form that corresponds directly to the definition of an algebraic addition theorem. We obtain

$$(w - uv)^2 - (1 - u^2)(1 - v^2) = 0,$$

or, finally,

$$w^2 - 2uvw + u^2 + v^2 - 1 = 0. \qquad (97)$$

Thus, in this case, $P(u, v, w) = w^2 - 2uvw + u^2 + v^2 - 1$, which is a third-degree polynomial.

We leave the reader to carry out the calculations for $\sin z$ independently.

34. The basic role of the addition theorems in the study and application of the exponential and trigonometric functions is well known. All the formulas in trigonometry are results of the addition theorems.

Let us show by some examples how one can obtain entire functions by starting with simple addition theorems.

a) $f(z_1 + z_2) = f(z_1) + f(z_2)$.

Let us first set $z_1 = z$ and $z_2 = 0$. This gives us $f(z) = f(z) + f(0)$, so that $f(0) = 0$.

Suppose now that $z_1 = z$ is a fixed point and that $z_2 = h \neq 0$ is a variable number. Then,

$$f(z + h) - f(z) = f(h) - f(0).$$

If we divide by h and take the limit as $h \to 0$, we obtain

$$f'(z) = f'(0) = C \equiv \text{const.}$$

Consequently,

$$f(z) = Cz + b.$$

Since $f(0) = 0$, we have $b = 0$. Finally,

$$f(z) = Cz,$$

that is, $f(z)$ is a linear function of z.

b) $[f(z_1 + z_2) - f(z_1) - f(z_2)]^2 - 4f(z_1)f(z_2) = 0$.

If we set $z_1 = z$ and $z_2 = 0$, we obtain

$$[f(0)]^2 - 4f(0)f(z) = 0,$$

from which we see that either $f(0) = 0$ or $f(z) = \frac{1}{4} f(0) \equiv \text{const}$, from which we get $f(z) \equiv 0$ (since, for $z = 0$, we obtain $f(0) = 4^{\frac{1}{4}} f(0)$ and, consequently, $f(0) = 0$).

Let us seek a solution of equation b) that is not identically 0. Then, for some $d \neq 0$, we must have $f(d) \neq 0$. Let us set $z_1 = z$ and $z_2 = d$ in b). We find

$$2\sqrt{f(d)}\,\sqrt{f(z)} = \pm\, [f(z + d) - f(d) - f(z)].$$

The right side of this equation is an entire function (since $f(z)$ and $f(z + d)$ are entire functions). Therefore, the left side and hence the function $\sqrt{f(z)}$ is an entire function. Let us set $\sqrt{f(z)} = \varphi(z)$.

From b), it follows that

$$f(z_1 + z_2) - f(z_1) - f(z_2) = 2\sqrt{f(z_1)}\,\sqrt{f(z_2)},$$
$$f(z_1 + z_2) = (\sqrt{f(z_1)} + \sqrt{f(z_2)})^2,$$

from which we get

$$\sqrt{f(z_1 + z_2)} = \sqrt{f(z_1)} + \sqrt{f(z_2)}$$

or

$$\varphi(z_1 + z_2) = \varphi(z_1) + \varphi(z_2).$$

We have shown that $\varphi(z)$ satisfies equation a). Therefore, $\varphi(z) = Cz$, and, since $f(z) = \varphi^2(z)$, we have

$$f(z) = C^2 z^2.$$

Here, for $C = 0$, we again obtain the solution $f(z) \equiv 0$ found above.

  c) $f(z_1 + z_2) = f(z_1)f(z_2)$.

  Let us first set $z_1 = z$ and $z_2 = 0$. We obtain $f(z) = f(z)f(0)$. If $f(0) \neq 1$, then $f(z) \equiv 0$. This is one of the solutions of equation c).

  Suppose now that $f(z) \not\equiv 0$. Then, $f(0) = 1$. If we set $z_1 = z$ and $z_2 = -z$, we obtain

$$f(0) = 1 = f(z)f(-z).$$

From this it follows that $f(z)$ does not vanish for any value of z. Consequently, $\operatorname{Ln} f(z)$ is an entire function (see Section 9). More precisely, there exists an entire function $g(z)$ such that

$$\operatorname{Ln} f(z) = g(z) + 2k\pi i \quad (k = 0, \pm 1, \pm 2, \ldots).$$

If we take the logarithm of both sides of c), we obtain

$$\operatorname{Ln} f(z_1 + z_2) = \operatorname{Ln} f(z_1) + \operatorname{Ln} f(z_2),$$

from which we get

$$g(z_1 + z_2) = g(z_1) + g(z_2).$$

Consequently,

$$g(z) = az, \quad \operatorname{Ln} f(z) = az + 2k\pi i \quad \text{and} \quad f(z) = e^{az + 2k\pi i} = e^{az}.$$

Thus, the only solutions of equation c) are $f(z) \equiv 0$ and $f(z) = e^{az}$, where a is an arbitrary complex constant.

  d) $[f(z_1 + z_2) - f(z_1)f(z_2)]^2 - [1 - f^2(z_1)][1 - f^2(z_2)] = 0$.

  If we set $z_1 = z$ and $z_2 = 0$, we obtain

$$f^2(z)[1 - f(0)]^2 - [1 - f^2(z)][1 - f^2(0)] = 0,$$

or

$$[1 - f(0)]\{2[f(z)]^2 - [1 + f(0)]\} = 0. \tag{98}$$

This relation will be satisfied if $[f(z)]^2 = [1 + f(0)]/2$ is a constant the value of which is determined by the equation

$$2 \, |f(0)|^2 - f(0) - 1 = 0.$$

Therefore,

$$f(0) = 1 \quad \text{or} \quad f(0) = -\frac{1}{2}.$$

Direct verification shows that both constants $f(z) \equiv 1$ and $f(z) \equiv -1/2$ satisfy equation d). Let us seek other solutions of this equation. As Eq. (98) shows, for such solutions, $f(0) = 1$.

At this point, we may proceed in different ways. Following one possible procedure, we reduce the question to equation c), which we have already considered; following a different procedure, we can obtain a differential equation that the unknown function must satisfy.

If $f(0) = 1$ and $f(z) \not\equiv 1$, then $f^2(z) \not\equiv 1$ and, consequently, there exists a value $z_2 = a$ such that $f^2(a) \neq 1$. In equation d), let us set $z_1 = z$ and $z_2 = a$, and let us rewrite the equation in the form

$$\sqrt{1 - [f(z)]^2} \ \sqrt{1 - [f(a)]^2} = \pm \, [f(z+a) - f(z) f(a)].$$

Since f is an entire function, the right side of this equation is an entire function. Hence, so is the left side and, since the second factor on the left is a constant, the first factor $\sqrt{1 - [f(z)]^2}$ is an entire function. Therefore, the function $f(z) + i \sqrt{1 - [f(z)]^2} = \varphi(z)$ must be an entire function. From equation d), we find*

$$f(z_1 + z_2) = f(z_1) f(z_2) - \sqrt{1 - [f(z_1)]^2} \ \sqrt{1 - [f(z_2)]^2}$$

or, after some simple manipulations,

$$\sqrt{1 - [f(z_1 + z_2)]^2} = $$
$$= f(z_1) \sqrt{1 - [f(z_2)]^2} + f(z_2) \sqrt{1 - [f(z_1)]^2}.$$

Consequently,

$$\varphi(z_1 + z_2) = f(z_1 + z_2) + i \sqrt{1 - [f(z_1 + z_2)]^2} = $$
$$= \{ f(z_1) f(z_2) - \sqrt{1 - [f(z_1)]^2} \ \sqrt{1 - [f(z_2)]^2} \} + $$
$$+ i \, \{ f(z_1) \sqrt{1 - [f(z_2)]^2} + f(z_2) \sqrt{1 - [f(z_1)]^2} \} = $$
$$= \{ f(z_1) + i \sqrt{1 - [f(z_1)]^2} \} \{ f(z_2) + i \sqrt{1 - [f(z_2)]^2} \} = $$
$$= \varphi(z_1) \, \varphi(z_2).$$

---

*If we take the plus sign in front of the product of the two radicals, then, for $z_1 = z_2 = z$, we obtain $f(2z) = 1$, from which we get $f(z) \equiv 1$. We are now excluding this possibility.

We have shown that the entire function $\varphi(z)$ satisfies equation c). Therefore, there are two possibilities: Either $\varphi(z) \equiv 0$ (which must be ruled out since it would then follow that $[f(z)]^2 = [f(z)]^2 - 1$ or $\varphi(z) = e^{az}$. From $f(z) + i\sqrt{1 - [f(z)]^2} = e^{az}$, we conclude that

$$f(z) - i\sqrt{1 - [f(z)]^2} = 1 : |f(z) + i\sqrt{1 - [f(z)]^2}| = e^{-az}$$

and, consequently, $f(z) = (e^{az} + e^{-az})/2$ or, setting $a = \alpha i$,

$$f(z) = \frac{e^{i\alpha z} + e^{-i\alpha z}}{2} = \cos(\alpha z).$$

For $\alpha = 0$, we again obtain $f(z) \equiv 1$.

Thus, equation d) is satisfied by the two constants $-1/2$ and 1 and by trancendental entire functions of the form $\cos(\alpha z)$, where $\alpha \neq 0$.

It is interesting to consider another possible method of solving the problem. We again seek a solution $f(z) \not\equiv \text{const}$. Then, as we saw above, $f(0) = 1$. If we set $z_1 = -z_2 = z$, in d), we obtain

$$[1 - f(z)f(-z)]^2 - \{1 - [f(z)]^2\}\{1 - [f(-z)]^2\} = 0,$$

or

$$[f(z) - f(-z)]^2 = 0, \text{ so that } f(-z) = f(z).$$

Thus, the function $f(z)$ must be an even function. From this it follows that the power series for $f(z)$ must contain only even powers of z:

$$f(z) = 1 + a_2 z^2 + a_4 z^4 + \dots,$$

so that, in particular, we conclude that $f'(0) = 0$.

Finally, let us set $z_1 = z$ and $z_2 = h \neq 0$ in d) and let us rewrite the equation in the form

$$\{[f(z + h) - f(z)] - f(z)[f(h) - 1]\}^2 + \\ + \{1 - [f(z)]^2\}[f(h) - 1][f(h) + 1] = 0.$$

Noting that $1 = f(0)$, let us divide both sides by h^2. This yields

$$\left[\frac{f(z + h) - f(z)}{h} - f(z)\frac{f(h) - f(0)}{h}\right]^2 + \\ + \{1 - [f(z)]^2\}\frac{f(h) - 1}{h^2}[f(h) + 1] = 0.$$

Taking the limit as $h \to 0$ and noting that

$$\frac{f(z+h)-f(h)}{h} \to f'(z), \quad \frac{f(h)-f(0)}{h} \to f'(0)=0,$$

$$\frac{f(h)-1}{h^2} \to a_2, \quad f(h) \to 1,$$

we find

$$[f'(z)]^2 + 2a_2\{1 - [f(z)]^2\} = 0$$

or, differentiating,

$$2f'(z)f''(z) - 4a_2 f(z)f'(z) = 0.$$

Since $f'(z) \not\equiv 0$ (so that $f(z) \not\equiv$ const), we have

$$f''(z) - 2a_2 f(z) = 0.$$

This is a second-order linear differential equation with constant coefficients. Setting $2a_2 = -\alpha^2$ (where α is a complex number), we write its general solution in the form

$$f(z) = C_1 e^{\alpha i z} + C_2 e^{-\alpha i z}.$$

From the conditions $f(0) = 1$ and $f'(0) = 0$, we obtain $C_1 = C_2 = 1/2$. Therefore,

$$f(z) = \frac{e^{i\alpha z} + e^{-i\alpha z}}{2} = \cos \alpha z.$$

35. In the preceding sections, we encountered examples of functions possessing algebraic addition theorems. In addition to constant functions, we have looked at the linear function az, functions of the form az^n (for $n \geq 2$), the exponential function e^{az}, and the cosine and sine. The question arises as to whether every entire function obeys an algebraic addition theorem. The answer to this question may be somewhat surprising. It is given by the following

Theorem (Weierstrass). *If an entire function $f(z)$ obeys an algebraic addition theorem, it is either an algebraic polynomial (which as a special case may be constant) or a trigonometric polynomial.*

Thus, any such function can be represented either in the form

$$f(z) = a_0 + a_1 z + \ldots + a_n z^n,$$

or in the form

$$f(z) = a_0 + [a_1 \cos (\alpha z) + b_1 \sin (\alpha z)] + [a_2 \cos (2\alpha z) +$$
$$+ b_2 \sin (2\alpha z)] + \ldots + [a_n \cos (n\alpha z) + b_n \sin (n\alpha z)].$$

Of course, all the particular cases that we have encountered up to the present satisfy these requirements. To see that the exponential function $e^{\alpha z}$ can be regarded as a trigonometric polynomial, we need only apply Euler's formula to write it in the form

$$e^{\alpha z} = \cos (- \alpha i z) + i \sin (- \alpha i z) = \cos (\alpha i z) - i \sin (\alpha i z).$$

If we seek functions obeying an algebraic addition theorem in the class of meromorphic functions (see Section 26), which is broader than the class of entire functions, we find the following result (also due to Weierstrass):

The only functions that obey an algebraic addition theorem are rational functions, periodic functions that can be represented in the form of the quotient of two trigonometric polynomials (a special case of which are the functions $\tan z = (\sin z)/(\cos z)$ and $\cot z = (\cos z)/(\sin z)$), *and doubly-periodic (that is, elliptic) functions.* Further consideration of this subject would take us beyond the scope of the present book.

Appendix

§1. Picard's little theorem

1. To begin with, we need some extra information regarding the maximum absolute value and the order of an entire function.

We shall prove the so-called principle of the maximum absolute value (which is valid for any analytic function though, for simplicity of exposition, we shall confine ourselves to entire functions):

The absolute value $|f(z)|$ of a nonconstant entire function $f(z)$ does not have a maximum at any point in the complex plane.

Proof: Let z_0 denote an arbitrary point in the plane. If $f(z_0) = 0$, then, as we know, there exists a disk with center at z_0 in which $f(z)$ has no other zeros (see Section 21). This means that, everywhere in this disk, $|f(z)| > |f(z_0)| = 0$, for $z \neq z_0$. Therefore, $|f(z)|$ does not have a maximum at z_0.

Suppose now that $f(z_0) \neq 0$. Let us expand the function in a series of powers of $z - z_0$. We obtain the everywhere-convergent series

$$f(z) = f(z_0) + b_1(z - z_0) + \ldots + b_n(z - z_0)^n + \ldots .$$

Some of the coefficients b_n (for $n = 1, 2, \ldots$) in this series must be nonzero because, otherwise, $f(z)$ would be identically equal to the constant $f(z_0)$. Let b_k be the first nonzero coefficient in the series. Then,

$$f(z) = f(z_0) + b_k(z - z_0)^k + b_{k+1}(z - z_0)^{k+1} + \ldots \quad (b_k \neq 0). \qquad (1)$$

Let us rewrite (1) in the form

$$f(z) = f(z_0) + b_k(z-z_0)^k + b_k(z-z_0)^k \left[\frac{b_{k+1}}{b_k}(z-z_0) + \right.$$
$$\left. + \frac{b_{k+2}}{b_k}(z-z_0)^2 + \dots \right]. \qquad (1')$$

Through the point z_0, we can draw a ray L such that for all other points z on that ray, $\mathrm{Arg}\,[b_k(z-z_0)^k]$ will coincide with $\mathrm{Arg}\,f(z_0)$. In other words, the vectors $b_k(z-z_0)^k$ and $f(z_0)$ will be parallel with the same positive direction (see Fig. 5, a and b).

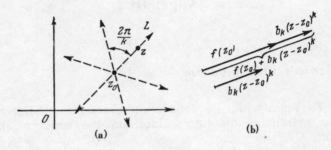

(a)   (b)

FIG. 5

We need only note that

$$\mathrm{Arg}\,[b_k(z-z_0)^k] = \mathrm{Arg}\,b_k + k\,\mathrm{Arg}\,(z-z_0),$$

and, consequently, the conditions stated will be satisfied if we take

$$\mathrm{Arg}\,b_k + k\,\mathrm{Arg}\,(z-z_0) = \mathrm{Arg}\,f(z_0),$$

that is,

$$\mathrm{Arg}\,(z-z_0) = \frac{\mathrm{Arg}\,f(z_0) - \mathrm{Arg}\,b_k}{k}.$$

(The reader can show for himself that this condition is satisfied by k distinct rays any one of which we may take as L [see Fig. 5, a].)

Obviously, the sum of $f(z_0)$ and $b_k(z-z_0)^k$ will then be greater in absolute value than $|f(z_0)|$ by an amount $|b_k(z-z_0)^k|$. But formula $(1')$ shows that, to get $f(z)$, we need to add to that sum one more term

$$\varphi(z) = b_k(z-z_0)^k \left[\frac{b_{k+1}}{b_k}(z-z_0) + \dots \right].$$

Since

$$\frac{\varphi(z)}{b_k(z-z_0)^k} = \frac{b_{k+1}}{b_k}(z-z_0) + \frac{b_{k+2}}{b_k}(z-z_0)^n + \ldots \to 0$$

as $z \to z_0$, we may assume that z is so close to z_0 that $\varphi(z)/$ $b_k(z-z_0)^k | < 1/2$, and this means that although the addition of $\varphi(z)$ to the sum $f(z_0) + b_k(z-z_0)^k$ may decrease the absolute value of that sum, it can do so by only half the absolute value of the second term. Thus, at points z lying on L and sufficiently close to z_0, we have

$$|f(z)| = |f(z_0) + b_k(z-z_0)^k + \varphi(z)| \geqq |f(z_0) + b_k(z-z_0)^k| -$$
$$- |\varphi(z)| = |f(z_0)| + |b_k(z-z_0)^k| - |\varphi(z)| > |f(z_0)| +$$
$$+ |b_k(z-z_0)^k| - \frac{1}{2}|b_k(z-z_0)^k| > |f(z_0)|. \tag{2}$$

From this inequality, we conclude that $|f(z)|$ cannot have a maximum at the point z_0. This completes the proof of the theorem.

From this theorem, we get the important

Corollary. If $f(z)$ is an entire function, then, for any $r > 0$, the maximum absolute value of $f(z)$ in the disk $|z| \leqslant r$ is attained at a point lying on the circle $|z| = r$.

Proof: If $f(z) \equiv$ const, its absolute value is also constant and hence the maximum absolute value coincides with the absolute value at an arbitrary point in the plane, in particular, with that at an arbitrary point on the circle $|z| = r$.

Suppose now that $f(z) \not\equiv$ const. Since $|f(z)|$ is a continuous function of z (which in turn follows from the continuity of $f(z)$), it follows from a well-known theorem of analysis that the maximum value of $|f(z)|$ in the disk $|z| \leqslant r$ is attained at some point z_0 in that disk. But, from what we have shown above, this point cannot lie in the interior of the circle (because otherwise $|f(z)|$ would have a maximum at that point). Consequently, z_0 lies on the boundary of the disk, that is, on the circle $|z_0| = r$.

Thus, the value of $M(r)$, that is, the maximum absolute value of $f(z)$ in the disk $|z| \leqslant r$, is one of the values of $|f(z)|$ at points of the circle $|z| = r$ and, consequently, coincides with the maximum absolute value of $f(z)$ on the circle $|z| = r$.

2. Let us establish certain inequalities for the coefficients of a power series that are analogous to Cauchy's inequality (see Section 10 of the main part of the text) except that they involve the maximum of the real part of the function instead of the maximum absolute value.

Suppose that $f(z)$ is an entire function

$$f(z) = a_0 + a_1 z + a_2 z^2 + \ldots + a_n z^n + \ldots \,. \tag{3}$$

Let us denote by α_n and β_n the real and imaginary parts of a_n respectively (so that $a_n = \alpha_n + i\beta_n$) and let us represent z in trigonometrical form:

$$z = r\,(\cos\theta + i\,\sin\theta) \qquad (r \geqslant 0).$$

We then obtain

$$f(z) = \sum_0^\infty (\alpha_n + i\beta_n)\,r^n\,(\cos n\theta + i\,\sin n\theta).$$

We can now represent the real part of $f(z)$, which we denote by $u\,(r,\ \theta)$, by the following series:

$$u\,(r,\ \theta) = \alpha_0 + \sum_1^\infty (\alpha_n \cos n\theta - \beta_n \sin n\theta)\,r^n. \tag{4}$$

If we fix r and integrate both sides with respect to θ from 0 to 2π, we obtain

$$\alpha_0 = \frac{1}{2\pi} \int_0^{2\pi} u\,(r,\ \theta)\,d\theta. \tag{5}$$

In an analogous manner, we can represent the remaining coefficients in the series (4) in the form of integrals. For example, compute α_p (with $p \geqslant 1$), we multiply both sides of (4) by $\cos p\theta$ and integrate from 0 to 2π. Then, we obtain on the left $\int_0^{2\pi} u\,(r,\ \theta)\cos p\theta\,d\theta$; on the right, all the integrals vanish except the integral $\int_0^{2\pi} \cos^2 p\theta\,d\theta = \pi$. Therefore,

$$\int_0^{2\pi} u\,(r,\ \theta)\cos p\theta\,d\theta = \alpha_p r^p \int_0^{2\pi} \cos^2 p\theta\,d\theta = \pi\alpha_p\,r^p,$$

so that

$$\alpha_p\,r^p = \frac{1}{\pi} \int_0^{2\pi} u\,(r,\ \theta)\cos p\theta\,d\theta \qquad (p = 1, 2, 3, \ldots). \tag{6}$$

Analogously, if we multiply both sides of (4) by $\sin p\theta$ and integrate, we obtain

$$\beta_p\,r^p = \frac{1}{\pi} \int_0^{2\pi} u\,(r,\ \theta)\sin p\theta\,d\theta \qquad (p = 1, 2, 3, \ldots). \tag{7}$$

From formulas (5)-(7), we conclude that

$$2\alpha_0 \pm \alpha_p r^p = \frac{1}{\pi} \int_0^{2\pi} u(r,\ \theta)(1 \pm \cos p\theta)\, d\theta, \tag{6'}$$

$$2\alpha_0 \pm \beta_p r^p = \frac{1}{\pi} \int_0^{2\pi} u(r,\ \theta)(1 \pm \sin p\theta)\, d\theta. \tag{7'}$$

The advantage of these formulas over formulas (6) and (7) is that the coefficients of $u(r,\ \theta)$ in the integrands are now nonnegative.

Let us denote by $\mu(r)$: the maximum $u(r,\ \theta)$ on the circle of radius r:

$$\mu(r) = \max_{0 \leqslant \theta \leqslant 2\pi} u(r,\ \theta).$$

From formulas $(6')$ and $(7')$, we obtain

$$2\alpha_0 \pm \alpha_p r^p \leqslant \frac{\mu(r)}{\pi} \int_0^{2\pi} (1 \pm \cos p\theta)\, d\theta = 2\mu(r),$$

$$2\alpha_0 \pm \beta_p r^p \leqslant 2\mu(r)$$

and, consequently,

$$|\alpha_p| \leqslant \frac{2\,[\mu(r) - \alpha_0]}{r^p},\ \ |\beta_p| \leqslant \frac{2\,[\mu(r) - \alpha_0]}{r^p} \quad (p = 1, 2, 3, \ldots). \tag{8}$$

We shall now prove the following theorem, which is a further generalization of Liouville's theorem (see Section 14 of the main text):

If the real part $u(r,\ \theta)$ of an entire function $f(z)$ satisfies the inequality

$$u(r,\ \theta) \leqslant \mu(r) \leqslant Cr^\delta \qquad (\delta > 0) \tag{9}$$

for all sufficiently large values of r (where $r > r_0$), then $f(z)$ must be a polynomial of degree not exceeding $n = [\delta]$ (where $[\delta]$ denotes the greatest integer not exceeding δ).

Proof: It follows from inequalities (8) and (9) that

$$|\alpha_p| \leqslant \frac{2\,(Cr^\delta - \alpha_0)}{r^p}, \qquad |\beta_p| \leqslant \frac{2\,(Cr^\delta - \alpha_0)}{r^p} \qquad (r > r_0). \tag{8'}$$

If $p > [\delta]$, it follows, since p is an integer, that $p \geqslant [\delta] + 1 > \delta$. Therefore, the expressions on the right sides of inequalities $(8')$ approach zero as $r \to \infty$. Consequently, $\alpha_p = \beta_p = 0$; that is, $a_p = \alpha_p + i\beta_p = 0$ if $p > [\delta] = n$. Therefore, formula (3) takes the form

$$f(z) = a_0 + a_1 z + \ldots + a_n z^n, \quad \text{where} \quad n = [\delta],$$

which completes the proof of the theorem.

3. We shall now prove three lemmas involving the calculation of the order of an entire function.

Lemma 1. If $f(z)$ is a transcendental entire function and $P(z)$ and $Q(z)$ are polynomials of degrees m and n, respectively, with $P(z) \not\equiv 0$, then the order ρ_1 of the function $P(z)f(z) + Q(z)$ coincides with the order ρ of the function $f(z)$; that is, $\rho_1 = \rho$.

Proof: We introduce the notations

$$M(r) = \max_{|z| \leqslant r} |f(z)|, \quad M_1(r) = \max_{|z| \leqslant r} |P(z)f(z) + Q(z)|. \quad (10)$$

From what was shown in Section 2, we do not need to consider points lying in the interior of the disk $|z| \leqslant r$ and may confine ourselves to the absolute values of the functions at points on the circle $|z| = r$.

Let $a_m z^m$ and $b_n z^n$ denote, respectively, the leading terms in the polynomials $P(z)$ and $Q(z)$. Then, on the basis of inequalities (28) of the main text, we may assert (taking $\varepsilon = 1/2$) that, for $|z| = r > r_0$

$$\left. \begin{aligned} \frac{1}{2}|a_m|r^m &\leqslant |P(z)| \leqslant \frac{3}{2}|a_m|r^m, \\ \frac{1}{2}|b_n|r^n &\leqslant |Q(z)| \leqslant \frac{3}{2}|b_n|r^n. \end{aligned} \right\} \quad (11)$$

Let z_0 denote a point on the circle $|z| = r$ at which $|f(z)|$ attains its maximum $M(r)$. Then,

$$M_1(r) \geqslant |P(z_0)f(z_0) + Q(z_0)| \geqslant |P(z_0)||f(z_0)| - |Q(z_0)| \geqslant$$
$$\geqslant \frac{1}{2}|a_m|r^m M(r) - \frac{3}{2}|b_n|r^n. \quad (12)$$

On the other hand, at the point z_1 (on the same circle) at which $|P(z)f(z) + Q(z)|$ attains the value $M_1(r)$, we have

$$M_1(r) = |P(z_1)f(z_1) + Q(z_1)| \leqslant |P(z_1)||f(z_1)| + |Q(z_1)| \leqslant$$
$$\leqslant \frac{3}{2}|a_m|r^m M(r) + \frac{3}{2}|b_n|r^n. \quad (13)$$

Consequently,

$$\frac{1}{2}|a_m|r^m M(r)\left[1 - \frac{3|b_n|r^n}{|a_m|r^m M(r)}\right] \leqslant M_1(r) \leqslant$$
$$\leqslant \frac{3}{2}|a_m|r^m M(r)\left[1 + \frac{|b_n|r^n}{|a_m|r^m M(r)}\right]. \quad (14)$$

Since $f(z)$ is a transcendental entire function, it follows (see Section 15 of the main text) that $M(r)$ increases faster than does the maximum absolute value of any polynomial and hence faster than any power of r. Therefore, each of the expressions in the square brackets in inequalities (14) approaches 1 as $r \to \infty$. Consequently, we may take r sufficiently large that the parenthetical expression on the right will, for example, be less than 2 and the parenthetical expression on the left will be greater than 2/3. Then,

$$\frac{1}{3} |a_m| r^m M(r) \leqslant M_1(r) \leqslant 3 |a_m| r^m M(r). \tag{15}$$

We recall that the order of an entire function $f(z)$ is

$$\varlimsup_{r \to \infty} \frac{\ln \ln M(r; f)}{\ln r} = \rho$$

(see Section 17 of the main text). If we take the logarithms of both sides of (15), we obtain

$$\ln \left(\frac{1}{3} |a_m| r^m \right) + \ln M(r) < \ln M_1(r) < \ln (3 |a_m| r^m) + \ln M(r),$$

or

$$\ln M(r) \left[1 + \frac{\ln \left(\frac{1}{3} |a_m| \right) + \ln (r^m)}{\ln M(r)} \right] <$$
$$< \ln M_1(r) < \ln M(r) \left[1 + \frac{\ln (3 |a_m|) + \ln (r^m)}{\ln M(r)} \right]. \tag{16}$$

Let us show that the expressions in the square brackets again approach 1 as $r \to \infty$. Obviously, it will be sufficient if we show that expressions of the form $\ln C + \ln (r^m) / \ln M(r)$, where $C \neq 0$, approach 0 as $r \to \infty$. For the term $\ln C / \ln M(r)$, this is obvious (since $\ln M(r) \to \infty$). Now, let ε denote an arbitrary positive number. Let us take a natural number N sufficiently great that $1/N < \varepsilon$, and let us choose $r_0 > 1$ such that, for all $r > r_0$, we have $r^{mN} / M(r) < 1$. (This is possible since $M(r)$ is the maximum-absolute-value function corresponding to the transcendental entire function $f(z)$.) Then, $r^{mN} < M(r)$, $N \ln(r^m) < \ln M(r)$, and $\ln (r^m) / \ln M(r) < 1/N < \varepsilon$. Thus, the ratio $[\ln (r^m)] / [\ln M(r)] \to 0$ as $r \to \infty$. From this it follows that, for all sufficiently large values of r in inequality (16), the bracketed expression on the right will be less than 2 and the bracketed expression on the left will be greater than 1/2. Thus,

$$\frac{1}{2} \ln M(r) < \ln M_1(r) < 2 \ln M(r).$$

If we again take the logarithms, we obtain

$$\ln \frac{1}{2} + \ln \ln M(r) < \ln \ln M_1(r) < \ln 2 + \ln \ln M(r).$$

If we divide by $\ln r$ and take the limits superior as $r \to \infty$, we have

$$\varlimsup_{r \to \infty} \frac{\ln \ln M(r)}{\ln r} \leqslant \varlimsup_{r \to \infty} \frac{\ln \ln M_1(r)}{\ln r} \leqslant \varlimsup_{r \to \infty} \frac{\ln \ln M(r)}{\ln r},$$

or

$$\rho \leqslant \rho_1 \leqslant \rho.$$

Thus, $\rho = \rho_1$. Consequently, we have shown that the orders of the functions $f(z)$ and $P(z)f(z) + Q(z)$ (where $P(z) \not\equiv 0$) are equal.

Lemma 2. The order of an entire function

$$f(z) = P(z) e^{g(z)} + Q(z),$$

where $P(z)$, $Q(z)$ and $g(z)$ are polynomials and $P(z)$ is not the zero polynomial, is equal to the degree of $g(z)$.

Proof: On the basis of Lemma 1, the order of $f(z)$ coincides with the order of the function $\varphi(z) = e^{g(z)}$. We need to show that

$$\varlimsup_{r \to \infty} \frac{\ln \ln M_1(r)}{\ln r} = n$$

where $\max_{|z|=r} |\varphi(z)| = M_1(r)$ and n is the degree of $g(z)$. Let us set

$$g(z) = c_0 + c_1 z + \ldots + c_n z^n,$$

$$c_k = \rho_k (\cos \alpha_k + i \sin \alpha_k),$$

$$z = r (\cos \theta + i \sin \theta).$$

By hypothesis, $\rho_n = |c_n| \neq 0$.

We then have

$$g(z) = \sum_{k=0}^{n} \rho_k r^k (\cos \alpha_k + i \sin \alpha_k)(\cos k\theta + i \sin k\theta) =$$

$$= \sum_{k=0}^{n} \rho_k r^k [\cos (\alpha_k + k\theta) + i \sin (\alpha_k + k\theta)].$$

To obtain the absolute value of $\varphi(z)$, we need only keep the exponential of the real part of this last expression:

$$|\varphi(z)| = e^{\sum_{k=0}^{n} \rho_k r^k \cos (\alpha_k + k\theta)}$$

and

$$\ln |\varphi(z)| = \sum_{k=0}^{n} \rho_k r^k \cos (\alpha_k + k\theta).$$

Obviously, by finding the maximum of this last expression with r constant and $0 \leqslant \theta \leqslant 2\pi$, we obtain

$$\ln \max_{|z|=r} |\varphi(z)|.$$

But

$$\ln |\varphi(z)| \leqslant \sum_{0}^{n} \rho_k r^k = \rho_n r^n \Big(1 + \frac{\rho_{n-1}}{\rho_n} \frac{1}{r} + \ldots + \frac{\rho_0}{\rho_n} \frac{1}{r^n} \Big)$$

and, consequently, for arbitrary ε in $(0, 1)$ and $r > r(\varepsilon)$, we have

$$\ln |\varphi(z)| < \rho_n r^n (1 + \varepsilon).$$

From this we get

$$\ln M_1(r) < \rho_n r^n (1 + \varepsilon).$$

Let z_0 denote a point on the circle $|z| = r$ such that $\cos (\alpha_n + n\theta) = 1$. (There are n such points, any one of which will serve our purpose.) We have

$$\ln M_1(r) \geqslant \ln |\varphi(z_0)| = \rho_n r^n + \sum_{0}^{n-1} \rho_k r^k \cos (\alpha_k + k\theta_0) \geqslant$$

$$\geqslant \rho_n r^n - \sum_{0}^{n-1} \rho_k r^k = \rho_n r^n \Big[1 - \Big(\frac{\rho_{n-1}}{\rho_n} \frac{1}{r} + \ldots + \frac{\rho_0}{\rho_n} \frac{1}{r^n} \Big) \Big] >$$

$$> \rho_n r^n (1 - \varepsilon) \qquad \text{for } r > r(\varepsilon).$$

Comparing the two inequalities that we have obtained, we conclude that

$$\rho_n r^n (1-\varepsilon) < \ln M_1(r) < \rho_n r^n (1+\varepsilon).$$

Taking the logarithms again, dividing by $\ln r$, and taking the limit as $r \to \infty$, we find

$$\lim_{r \to \infty} \frac{\ln \ln M_1(r)}{\ln r} = n.$$

Consequently, the order of $\varphi(z)$ is equal to n and hence, so is the order of the function $f(z)$.

Lemma 3. If $g(z)$ is an entire function and if the order of the function $f(z) = e^{g(z)}$ is finite, then $g(z)$ is a polynomial and hence the order of $f(z)$ is an integer.

If $z = r(\cos\theta + i\sin\theta)$ and if $u(r,\theta)$ is the real part of the function $g(z)$, then $|f(z)| = e^{u(r,\theta)}$, so that $\ln|f(z)| = u(r,\theta)$.

We denote $\max\limits_{|z|=r}|f(z)| = M(r)$ and $\max\limits_{0\leq\theta\leq 2\pi} u(r,\theta) = \mu(r)$. Then,

$$\ln M(r) = \mu(r). \tag{17}$$

Suppose that δ is the order of $f(z)$. This means that

$$\varlimsup_{r \to \infty} \frac{\ln \ln M(r)}{\ln r} = \delta.$$

For arbitrary $\varepsilon > 0$, there exists an $r(\varepsilon) > 1$ such that, for $r > r(\varepsilon)$,

$$\frac{\ln \ln M(r)}{\ln r} < \delta + \varepsilon;$$

that is,

$$\ln \ln M(r) < \ln(r^{\delta + \varepsilon})$$

or

$$\ln M(r) < r^{\delta + \varepsilon}. \tag{18}$$

From (17) and (18), it follows that

$$\mu(r,\theta) < r^{\delta+\varepsilon}, \quad r > r(\varepsilon).$$

From the theorem in Section 2 of this portion of the Appendix, it follows that $g(z)$ is a polynomial, the degree n of which does not exceed the real part of $\delta + \varepsilon$; that is, $n \leqslant |\delta + \varepsilon|$. Since ε is arbitrarily small, it follows that $n \leqslant |\delta|$. From Lemma 2, the order δ of the function $f(z)$ must coincide with n. Therefore, δ is an integer:

$$\delta = n.$$

This completes the proof of Lemma 3.

4. It is now easy to prove the little Picard theorem for the case of entire functions of finite order. We shall prove it in a more general form, considering not the equation $f(z) = A$ but the equation $f(z) = AP(z)$, where $P(z)$ is a polynomial. Let us first suppose that the order of the entire function is not an integer.

Theorem 1. Let $f(z)$ denote a transcendental entire function the order δ which is finite but not an integer. Then, if $P(z)$ is a nonzero polynomial, the equation

$$f(z) = AP(z)$$

has infinitely many roots for arbitrary A (with no exception).

Proof:(by contradiction): Let us suppose that there exists an $A = A_0$ for which Eq. (19) has only finitely many roots if any at all.

Then, the entire function $f(z) - A_0 P(z)$ has only finitely many zeros. According to Section 20 of the main text, we may then represent the function $f(z) - A_0 P(z)$ in the form

$$f(z) - A_0 P(z) = Q(z) e^{g(z)}, \tag{20}$$

so that

$$f(z) = A_0 P(z) + Q(z) e^{g(z)}. \tag{21}$$

Here, $Q(z)$ is a nonzero polynomial (it may be taken identically equal to 1 if the equation $f(z) - A_0 P(z) = 0$ has no roots) and $g(z)$ is some entire function.

From Lemma 1 of the preceding section, the order δ of the function $f(z)$ must coincide with the order of the function $e^{g(z)}$ and, consequently, it must, in accordance with Lemma 3, be an integer, which contradicts the hypothesis of the theorem. Thus, Theorem 1 is proven.

Let us return to entire functions of finite integral order. For such functions we have

Theorem 2. If $f(z)$ is a transcendental entire function of finite integral order n and if $P(z)$ is a nonzero polynomial, the equation

$$f(z) = AP(z) \tag{22}$$

has infinitely many roots for arbitrary A with the possible exception of one value.

Proof:(by contradiction): Suppose that there exist at least two distinct values a and b at which Eq. (22) has only finitely many roots. This means that the entire functions $f(z) - aP(z)$ and $f(z) - bP(z)$ have only finitely many zeros. We may therefore assert (see Section 20 of the main text) that

$$f(z) - aP(z) = Q_1(z) e^{g_1(z)}, \quad f(z) - bP(z) = Q_2(z) e^{g_2(z)}, \tag{23}$$

where $Q_1(z)$ and $Q_2(z)$ are nonzero polynomials and $g_1(z)$ and $g_2(z)$ are entire functions. It follows from Lemma 1 of Section 3 that the orders of $e^{g_1(z)}$ and $e^{g_2(z)}$ coincide with the order n of $f(z)$.

On the basis of Lemmas 3 and 2 of Section 3, we conclude that the functions $g_1(z)$ and $g_2(z)$ must be polynomials of degree n. It then follows, in particular, that we may take $n \geqslant 1$ since, for $n = 0$, the functions $g_1(z)$ and $g_2(z)$ would be constants and it would follow from formulas (23) that $f(z)$ is a polynomial and not a transcendental entire function. Let us subtract the second of Eqs. (23) from the first:

$$Q_1(z) e^{g_1(z)} - Q_2(z) e^{g_2(z)} = (b - a) P(z) = p(z), \tag{24}$$

where the polynomial $p(z) = (b - a) P(z)$ is not the zero polynomial (since $b \neq a$ and $P(z) \not\equiv 0$). Our purpose is to show that such an identity is impossible if the polynomials $Q_1(z,)$, $Q_2(z)$, and $p(z)$ are not the zero polynomial and $g_1(z)$ and $g_2(z)$ are polynomials of degree $\geqslant 1$. Differentiating (24), we obtain

$$[Q_1'(z) + Q_1(z) g_1'(z)] e^{g_1(z)} - \\ - [Q_2'(z) + Q_2(z) g_2'(z)] e^{g_2(z)} = p'(z). \tag{25}$$

If we consider (24) and (25) as a system of equations in unknowns $e^{g_1(z)}$ and $e^{g_2(z)}$, then the determinant $\Delta(z)$ of the system will be

$$\Delta(z) = -Q_1(z)[Q_2'(z) + Q_2(z) g_2'(z)] + \\ + Q_2(z)[Q_1'(z) + Q_1(z) g_1'(z)] = Q_2(z) Q_1'(z) - Q_1(z) Q_2'(z) + \\ + Q_1(z) Q_2(z) [g_1'(z) - g_2'(z)]. \tag{26}$$

Let us show that the polynomial $\Delta(z) \not\equiv 0$. In the opposite case, by dividing both sides of the presumed identity $\Delta(z) \equiv 0$ by $Q_1(z) Q_2(z)$, we would obtain

$$\frac{Q_1'(z)}{Q_1(z)} - \frac{Q_2'(z)}{Q_2(z)} + [g_1(z) - g_2(z)]' = 0.$$

Integrating, we find

$$\mathrm{Ln}\, \frac{Q_1(z)}{Q_2(z)} + g_1(z) - g_2(z) \equiv \mathrm{const} = C_1, \tag{27}$$

so that

$$\frac{Q_1(z)}{Q_2(z)} e^{g_1(z) - g_2(z)} = e^{C_1} = C \neq 0. \tag{28}$$

But it follows from formulas (23) that

$$\frac{Q_1(z)}{Q_2(z)} e^{g_1(z) - g_2(z)} = \frac{f(z) - aP(z)}{f(z) - bP(z)}.$$

Therefore, formula (28) means that

$$\frac{f(z) - aP(z)}{f(z) - bP(z)} = C,$$

so that

$$(1 - C) f(z) = (a - bC) P(z).$$

Since $b \neq a$, we have $C \neq 1$ and hence

$$f(z) = \frac{a - bC}{1 - C} P(z),$$

which contradicts the hypothesis (since $f(z)$ is assumed to be a transcendental function). Thus, $\Delta(z) \not\equiv 0$. If we solve the system (24), (25) for $e^{g_1(z)}$ and $e^{g_2(z)}$ we obtain

$$e^{g_1(z)} = \frac{-p(z) [Q_2'(z) + Q_2(z) g_2'(z)] + p'(z) Q_2(z)}{\Delta(z)},$$

$$e^{g_2(z)} = \frac{p'(z) Q_1(z) - p(z) [Q_1'(z) + Q_1(z) g_1'(z)]}{\Delta(z)}.$$

But equations of this kind contain a contradiction since the function on the left is in each case a transcendental entire function (of order $n \geqslant 1$) and the function on the right is a rational function (and hence a polynomial since it is entire). This completes the proof of Theorem 2.

   5. Exept for the fact that Theorem 1 of the preceding section excludes the possibility of exceptional values under the conditions

stated, both Theorems 1 and 2 can be regarded as very special cases of the following theorem (also due to Picard).

Theorem. Let $\varphi(z)$ *denote a transcendental meromorphic function* (which, as a special case, may be an entire function). *For every complex number* A *(finite or infinite) with two possible exceptions, the equation*

$$\varphi(z) = A$$

has infinitely many roots.

Proof: If $\varphi(z)$ is an entire function, it does not become infinite at any z. Therefore, $A = \infty$ is one exceptional value for every entire function. Consequently, on the basis of the last theorem, in the case of a transcendental entire function, there may exist at most one finite exceptional value. Picard's little theorem also makes reference to this.

If $f(z)$ is a transcendental entire function and $P(z)$ is a non-zero polynomial, the meromorphic function $\varphi(z) = f(z)/P(z)$ becomes infinite only at a finite number of points (namely, the zeros of the polynomial $P(z)$). Therefore, as before, the value ∞ is an exceptional value for this function and, on the basis of the above theorem, still one other (finite) exceptional value is possible. Therefore, we may assert that the equation $f(z)/P(z) = A$, or $f(z) = AP(z)$, has infinitely many roots for every value of A except possibly a single finite value of A. For the case in which the order of $f(z)$ is finite, we proved this in Section 4 of this part of the Appendix (see Theorems 1 and 2).

Finally, let $f(z)$ and $g(z)$ denote two transcendental entire functions, the ratio of which is not a rational function. This means that $f(z)/g(z)$ is a transcendental meromorphic function. According to the above theorem, we may assert that $f(z)/g(z) = A$, that is, the equation $f(z) = Ag(z)$ has infinitely many roots for arbitrary A except for at most two values. This theorem was mentioned in Section 26 of the main text.

§2. Periodic entire functions. Weierstrass' theorem

6. In Section 30 of the main text, we cited the function $e^{\frac{2\pi i}{\omega} z}$ as the simplest example of a function with period $\omega \neq 0$. Let us set $t = e^{\frac{2\pi i}{\omega} z}$ and let us show that every periodic entire function $f(z)$ with period ω can be considered as a single-valued analytic function of t at all points of the complex t-plane except the point $t = 0$. We have $\operatorname{Ln} t = 2\pi i \omega / z$ and hence $z = (z/2\pi i) \operatorname{Ln} t$. For $t \neq 0$,

this is a multiple-valued analytic function of t. Since all values of $\operatorname{Ln} t$ for given t, differ by integral multiples of $2\pi i$, all the values of z corresponding to the same t differ from one another by integral multiples of ω. Therefore, they correspond to the same value of the periodic function $f(z)$. Consequently, $f(z)$ is a single-valued function of t in the entire complex plane except for the point $t=0$. We define

$$\varphi(t)=f(z)=f\left(\frac{\omega}{2\pi i}\operatorname{Ln} t\right). \tag{29}$$

From the chain rule for differentiating a composite function, we have

$$\varphi'(t)=f'(z)\frac{dz}{dt}=f'(z)\frac{\omega}{2\pi i}t^{-1},$$

that is, the derivative $\varphi'(t)$ exists at an arbitrary point $t\neq 0$. Therefore, $\varphi(t)$ is an analytic function at all points in the plane except the coordinate origin. For such functions, we have the following proposition from the general theory of analytic functions, which is a special case of Laurent's theorem:

If $\varphi(t)$ is a single-valued analytic function at all points of the complex plane except possibly the point $t=0$, it can be represented as the sum of an everywhere-convergent generalized power series (known as a Laurent *series) of the form*

$$\varphi(t)=\sum_{-\infty}^{+\infty}a_n t^n, \tag{30}$$

containing in general both nonnegative and negative powers of t.

If we apply to the series (30) the device used in Section 10 of the main text for expressing the coefficients in terms of integrals, we obtain the following formulas:

$$a_n=\frac{1}{2\pi}\int_0^{2\pi}\frac{\varphi(t)}{t^n}\,d\alpha; \tag{31}$$

where the point $t=r(\cos\alpha+i\sin\alpha)$ moves counterclockwise around the circle in the t-plane of radius r (where r is an arbitrary positive number) with center at the coordinate origin. Reasoning as in Section 10, we derive the inequalities

$$|a_n|\leqslant\frac{\mu(r)}{r^n},\quad n=0,\ \pm 1,\ \pm 2,\ \pm 3,\ldots, \tag{32}$$

where

$$\mu(r) = \max_{|t|=r} |\varphi(t)|. \tag{33}$$

In the present case,

$$t = e^{\frac{2\pi i}{\omega} z} \quad \text{and} \quad \varphi(t) = f\left(\frac{\omega}{2\pi i} \operatorname{Ln} t\right) = f(z).$$

Therefore, it follows from formula (30) that

$$f(z) = \sum_{-\infty}^{+\infty} a_n e^{\frac{2\pi i}{\omega} nz}. \tag{34}$$

Thus, an arbitrary periodic entire function $f(z)$ with period ω can be represented as the limit of an everywhere-convergent series of the form (34), the terms in which are periodic (exponential) functions with the same period ω. If we now replace $e^{2\pi i nz/\omega}$ by $\cos\left(\frac{2\pi}{\omega} nz\right) + i \sin\left(\frac{2\pi}{\omega} nz\right)$ and group the terms in a suitable order (which is permissible because of the absolute convergence of the series), we obtain a representation of $f(z)$ as the limit of a trigonometrical series:

$$f(z) = \sum_{0}^{\infty} \left[A_n \cos\left(\frac{2\pi}{\omega} nz\right) + B_n \sin\left(\frac{2\pi}{\omega} nz\right) \right]. \tag{35}$$

Let us prove the following fundamental theorem on periodic functions:

If a periodic entire function $f(z)$ with period ω satisfies an inequality of the form

$$|f(z)| \leqslant Ce^{\gamma \frac{2\pi}{|\omega|} |z|} \tag{36}$$

for certain $C > 0$ and $\gamma > 0$ and for all sufficiently large values of $|z|$ (where $|z| > R_0$), then $f(z)$ is a trigonometric polynomial of order not exceeding $p = [\gamma]$, where $[\gamma]$ is the greatest integer not exceeding γ.

Proof: We use inequalities (32), which are analogous to Cauchy's inequality for the coefficients of a power series.

We note that, in the present case,

$$\mu(r) = \max_{|t|=r} |\varphi(t)| = \max_{|t|=r} \left| f\left(\frac{\omega}{2\pi i} \operatorname{Ln} t\right) \right|.$$

To find a bound for this quantity with the aid of inequality (36), let us first look at the value of $(\omega/2\pi i)\,\mathrm{Ln}\,t$ for $|t|=r$, that is, for $t=r(\cos\alpha+i\sin\alpha)$, where $0\leqslant\alpha\leqslant2\pi$. We have

$$\frac{\omega}{2\pi i}\,\mathrm{Ln}\,t=\frac{\omega}{2\pi i}\,(\ln|t|+i\,\mathrm{Arg}\,t)=\frac{\omega}{2\pi i}\,[\ln r+i\,(\alpha+2\,k\pi)]=$$
$$=\frac{\alpha}{2\pi}\,\omega+k\omega+\frac{\omega}{2\pi i}\,\ln r.$$

Therefore,

$$f\Big(\frac{\omega}{2\pi i}\,\mathrm{Ln}\,t\Big)=f\Big(\frac{\alpha}{2\pi}\,\omega+k\,\omega+\frac{\omega}{2\pi i}\,\ln r\Big)=$$
$$=f\Big(\frac{\alpha}{2\pi}\,\omega+\frac{\omega}{2\pi i}\,\ln r\Big),$$

since $k\omega$ is a period of $f(z)$. Consequently,

$$\mu(r)=\max_{0\leqslant\alpha\leqslant2\pi}\Big|f\Big(\frac{\alpha}{2\pi}\,\omega+\frac{\omega}{2\pi i}\,\ln r\Big)\Big|. \tag{37}$$

If we set $z=\frac{\alpha}{2\pi}\,\omega+\frac{\omega}{2\pi i}\,\ln r$, we note that $|z|=\frac{|\omega|}{2\pi}|\ln r+i\alpha|$ will increase without bound not only as $r\to\infty$ but also as $r\to0$. Therefore, we may assume that $|z|>R_0$ either for sufficiently large $r>r_1>1$ or for sufficiently small $r<r_2<1$. In each of these cases, we may use inequality (36) to find a bound for $|f(z)|$. We find

$$|f(z)|\leqslant Ce^{\gamma|\ln r+i\alpha|}<Ce^{\gamma(|\ln r|+2\pi)},$$

since $0\leqslant\alpha\leqslant2\pi$. Let us set $Ce^{2\pi\gamma}=C_1$, and rewrite the above inequality in the form

$$|f(z)|<C_1e^{\gamma|\ln r|}. \tag{38}$$

If, for example, $r>r_1>1$, then $|\ln r|=\ln r$ and $e^{\gamma|\ln r|}=r^\gamma$. Consequently,

$$\mu(r)=\max|f(z)|<C_1r^\gamma$$

and, on the basis of (31),

$$|a_n|<\frac{C_1r^\gamma}{r^n}.$$

Obviously, if $n > p = [\gamma]$, then $n \geq [\gamma] + 1 > \gamma$. Therefore, as $r \to \infty$, the right side of the above inequality approaches zero. Consequently,

$$a_n = 0, \quad \text{if} \quad n > p, \text{ i.e.,} \quad a_{p+1} = a_{p+2} = a_{p+3} = \ldots = 0. \qquad (39)$$

Suppose now that $r < r_2 < 1$. Then, $|\ln r| = \ln(1/r)$, and inequality (38) assumes the form $|f(z)| < C_1 r^{-\gamma}$. Consequently, $\mu(r) = \max |f(z)| < C_1 r^{-\gamma}$. From (31),

$$|a_n| < \frac{C_1 r^{-\gamma}}{r^n} = C_1 r^{-n-\gamma}.$$

Let us assign to n negative values less than $-p = -[\gamma]$. Then, $n \leq -p - 1$. Since $p + 1 = [\gamma] + 1 > \gamma$, it follows that $-p - 1 < -\gamma$; that is, $n < -\gamma$ or $-n - \gamma > 0$. Therefore, $r^{-n-\gamma} \to 0$ as $r \to 0$ and, consequently, $a_n = 0$ if $n < -p$; that is,

$$a_{-p-1} = a_{-p-2} = a_{-p-3} = \ldots = 0. \qquad (40)$$

Keeping (39) and (40) in mind, we conclude that the infinite series (34) reduces to the finite sum

$$f(z) = \sum_{-p}^{+p} a_n e^{\frac{2\pi i}{\omega} nz}. \qquad (34')$$

If we now write $e^{\frac{2\pi i}{\omega} nz}$ in the form $\cos\left(\frac{2\pi}{\omega} nz\right) + i \sin\left(\frac{2\pi}{\omega} nz\right)$ and group terms of the same argument of sine or cosine (using the properties that the cosine is an even and the sine an odd function), we finally obtain

$$f(z) = a_0 + \left[A_1 \cos\left(\frac{2\pi}{\omega} z\right) + B_1 \sin\left(\frac{2\pi}{\omega} z\right) \right] + \ldots + $$
$$+ \left[A_p \cos\left(\frac{2\pi}{\omega} pz\right) + B_p \sin\left(\frac{2\pi}{\omega} pz\right) \right], \qquad (35')$$

which completes the proof.

We note that the converse theorem is also valid:

If $f(z)$ is a trigonometric polynomial of order p, that is, if

$$f(z) = \sum_{-p}^{p} a_n e^{\frac{2\pi i}{\omega} nz},$$

there exists a positive number C such that

$$|f(z)| < Ce^{p\frac{2\pi}{|\omega|}|z|}$$

for all z.

Proof: we have

$$|f(z)| \leqslant \sum_{-p}^{p} |a_n| e^{\frac{2\pi}{|\omega|}|n||z|} \leqslant \sum_{-p}^{p} |a_n| e^{\frac{2\pi}{|\omega|}p|z|} = Ce^{\frac{2\pi}{|\omega|}p|z|}, \qquad (41)$$

where $C = \sum_{-p}^{p} |a_n|$.

Therefore, a periodic function that does not satisfy the hypothesis of the fundamental theorem cannot be a trigonometric polynomial. Since in all cases it can be represented in the form of a series

$$f(z) = \sum_{-\infty}^{+\infty} a_n e^{\frac{2\pi i}{\omega}nz},$$

infinitely many of the coefficients a_n must be nonzero.

7. Let $f(z)$ denote an entire function. If it is a polynomial, it will obey an algebraic addition theorem. Specifically, in the system

$$\left.\begin{array}{l} u - f(z_1) = 0, \\ v - f(z_2) = 0, \\ w - f(z_1 + z_2) = 0 \end{array}\right\} \qquad (42)$$

we can eliminate the variables z_1 and z_2 by using one of the devices studied in higher algebra.* By doing so, we obtain an algebraic relationship between u, v and w:

$$P(u, v, w) = 0;$$

where $(P(u, v, w)$ is a polynomial.

Suppose now that $f(z)$ is a transcendental entire function. Let us show that if it obeys an algebraic addition theorem, this function must necessarily be periodic. This proposition constitutes the essential assertion in a theorem originally proven by Weierstrass.

---

*See, for example, A. G. Kurosh, *Kurs vysshey albebry* (Course in higher algebra), 7th ed., pp. 340-343.

As a preliminary, we prove the

Lemma. If $p_0(u, v) \not\equiv 0$ *is a nonzero polynomial in u and v, there exists infinitely many values of u at which* $p_0(u, v)$ *does not vanish identically in* v.

Proof. Suppose that

$$p_0(u, v) = q_0(u) v^m + q_1(u) v^{m-1} + \ldots + q_m(u),$$

where $q_0(u), \ldots, q_m(u)$ are polynomials and suppose that $q_0(u) \not\equiv 0$.

If the degree of $q_0(u)$ is s, there exist no more than s distinct values of u at which $q_0(u) = 0$. For each of the infinitely many values of u that are distinct from these s values, we have $q_0(u) \neq 0$. Consequently the polynomial

$$q_0(u) v^m + q_1(u) v^{m-1} + \ldots + q_m(u)$$

is not identically zero. This completes the proof of the lemma.

Suppose now that the addition theorem for $f(z)$ is of the form

$$P(u, v, w) = w^n p_0(u, v) + w^{n-1} p_1(u, v) + \\ + \ldots + p_n(u, v) = 0, \qquad (43)$$

where $p_0(u, v)$ [assumed not identically zero], $p_1(u, v), \ldots, p_n(u, v)$ are polynomials. On the basis of the above lemma, there exist infinitely many distinct values of u at which $p_0(u, v)$ is not the zero polynomial in v. Let a and b denote two such values. Then, on the basis of Picard's little theorem, at least one of the equations

$$f(z) = a \quad \text{or} \quad f(z) = b \qquad (a \neq b)$$

has infinitely many roots. Let us suppose that this is the case with the equation

$$f(z) = a. \qquad (44)$$

Then, we can exhibit $n + 1$ distinct roots of this equation, which we denote $c_1, c_2, \ldots, c_{n+1}$. Thus, $p_0(a, v) \not\equiv 0$ and $f(c_1) = f(c_2) = \ldots = f(c_{n+1}) = a$, where $c_1, c_2, \ldots, c_{n+1}$ are all distinct numbers.

If we set

$$u = f(c_j) = a, \quad v = f(z) \quad \text{and} \quad w = f(c_j + z),$$

in (43), we obtain

$$p_0 \left[a,\, f(z) \right] \left| \left[f(c_j + z) \right] \right.^n + p_1 \left[a,\, f(z) \right] \left[f(c_j + z) \right]^{n-1} +$$
$$+ \ldots + p_n \left[a,\, f(z) \right] = 0 \qquad (j = 1,\, 2, \ldots,\, n + 1). \qquad (43')$$

If $v = f(z)$ is distinct from the roots of the equation $p_0 (a,\, v) = 0$ (such a coincidence can happen at no more than t values of the function $f(z)$, where t is the degree of $p_0 (a,\, v)$ with respect to v so we can find a value of z for which $f(z)$ is different from any of these values), then $p_0 \left[a,\, f(z) \right] \neq 0$, and the equation

$$p_0 \left[a,\, f(z) \right] w^n + p_1 \left[a,\, f(z) \right] w^{n-1} + \ldots + p_n \left[a, f(z) \right] = 0 \qquad (43'')$$

is an nth-degree equation in w. Therefore, it has no more than n distinct roots. On the other hand, this equation must, on the basis of $(43')$, be satisfied by each of the $n + 1$ numbers

$$f(c_1 + z),\, f(c_2 + z), \ldots,\, f(c_{n+1} + z).$$

From this it follows that at least two of these numbers must coincide. Suppose, for example, that

$$f(c_j + z) = f(c_k + z), \quad c_k \neq c_j. \qquad (45)$$

If we take another value $z' \neq z$, it may be necessary to choose a different pair of indices j' and k', in which case, we obtain

$$f(c_{j'} + z') = f(c_{k'} + z'), \quad c_{k'} \neq c_{j'}.$$

Let us substitute for z an arbitrary point in the disk $|z| \leqslant 1$ such that $v = f(z)$ does not coincide with any of the t roots of the equation $p_0 (a,\, v) = 0$. Since there are only t points satisfying that equation, there are infinitely many admissible values of z and for each we have a pair of indices j and k in Eq. (45) such that $1 \leqslant j \leqslant n + 1$ and $1 \leqslant k \leqslant n + 1$. Since there are only finitely many (namely, $(n + 1)n / 2$) such possible pairs of distinct indices, at least one of the pairs, let us say, the pair $(j_0,\, k_0)$, will be repeated for infinitely many points z in the disk $|z| \leqslant 1$. Consequently, for infinitely many points z,

$$f(c_{j_0} + z) = f(c_{k_0} + z), \quad c_{k_0} \neq c_{j_0}, \qquad (45')$$

where the indices j_0 and k_0 do not vary with change in z. Since $f(c_{j_0} + z)$ and $f(c_{k_0} + z)$ are entire functions of z, the fact that their values coincide at infinitely many points in the disk $|z| \leqslant 1$ implies that they are identically equal to each other (cf. the uniqueness theorem for entire functions in Section 21 of the main text).

Thus,

$$f(c_j + z) \equiv f(c_{k_0} + z) \tag{45''}$$

or, by setting $c_{j_0} + z = \zeta$ and, consequently, $c_{k_0} + z = c_{k_0} - c_{j_0} + \zeta$, we have

$$f(\zeta) \equiv f[\zeta + (c_{k_0} - c_{j_0})]. \tag{46}$$

From this we see that $\omega = c_{k_0} - c_{j_0} \neq 0$ is a period of $f(z)$, that is, that $f(z)$ is a periodic function.

8. However, not every transcendental entire periodic function obeys an algebraic addition theorem. Weierstrass' theorem asserts further that such a function must be a trigonometric polynomial and, consequently, must obey an inequality of the form (36). This part of the theorem can be proven by following the same scheme as the part that we have proven but it requires a more profound familiarity with periodic functions and it rests not on the little but on the so-called great theorem of Picard. We note that, on the basis of Weierstrass' theorem in its complete statement, the periodic entire function e^{ez} (with period obviously $2\pi i$) does not obey an algebraic addition theorem simply because its maximum absolute value increases too rapidly (cf. Section 17 of the main text).

Finally, Weierstrass' theorem for entire functions can be formulated as follows:

Weierstrass' theorem. If a transcendental entire function $f(z)$ obeys an algebraic addition theorem, it is a trigonometric polynomial.

The converse is also true: *Every trigonometric polynomial obeys an algebraic addition theorem.*

Proof of converse: Suppose that

$$f(z) = \sum_{-p}^{p} a_n e^{\frac{2\pi i}{\omega} nz}, \tag{47}$$

where the a_n are complex coefficients. Taking two arbitrary complex numbers z_1 and z_2, we may write

$$\left. u = \sum_{-p}^{+p} a_n e^{\frac{2\pi i}{\omega} nz_1}, \quad v = \sum_{-p}^{+p} a_n e^{\frac{2\pi i}{\omega} nz_2}, \atop w = \sum_{-p}^{+p} a_n e^{\frac{2\pi i}{\omega} n(z_1 + z_2)} \right\} \tag{48}$$

For brevity, let us set $e^{\frac{2\pi i}{\omega} z_1} = t_1$ and $e^{\frac{2\pi i}{\omega} z_2} = t_2$. Then, the relations (48) become

$$u - \sum_{-p}^{+p} a_n t_1^n = 0, \quad v - \sum_{-p}^{+p} a_n t_2^n = 0, \quad w - \sum_{-p}^{+p} a_n t_1^n t_2^n = 0, \qquad (49)$$

and when we multiply through by t_1^p and/or t_2^p to eliminate negative powers of t_1 and t_2, they become

$$\left.\begin{array}{l} ut_1^p - (a_{-p} + a_{-p+1} t_1 + \ldots + a_p t_1^{2p}) = 0, \\ vt_2^p - (a_{-p} + a_{-p+1} t_2 + \ldots + a_p t_2^{2p}) = 0, \\ wt_1^p t_2^p - (a_{-p} + a_{-p+1} t_1 t_2 + \ldots + a_p t_2^{2p}) = 0. \end{array}\right\} \qquad (50)$$

From this system of three algebraic equations in the five variables t_1, t_2, u, v, and w, we can eliminate t_1 and t_2. When we do this, we obtain a single algebraic equation relating u, v, and w:

$$P(u, v, w) = 0.$$

This is the addition theorem for the trigonometric polynomial (47).

Index